STILL MOTION

Poems and Photographs

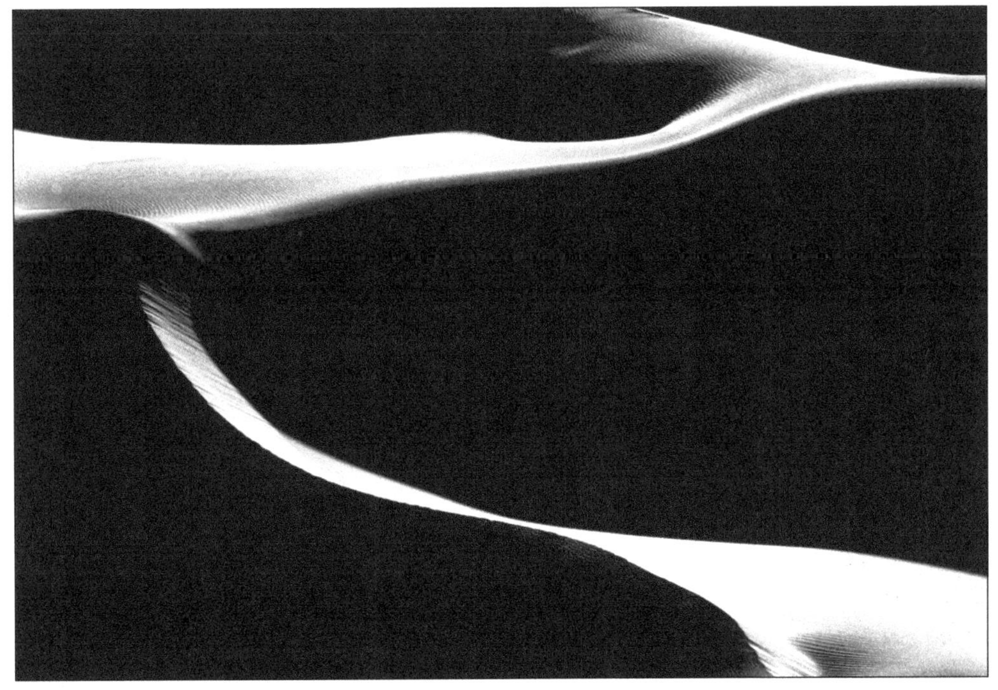

Jianqing Zheng - Poet
Leo Touchet - Photographer

STILL MOTION
Poems and Photographs

Jianqing Zheng, Poet
Leo Touchet, Photographer

Design by
Leo Touchet

Photos Copyright © 2025 Leo Touchet
Poems Copyright © 2025 Jianqing Zheng
All Rights Reserved

ISBN: 979-8-991-8323-2-1-1

Deluxe Edition
March 2025

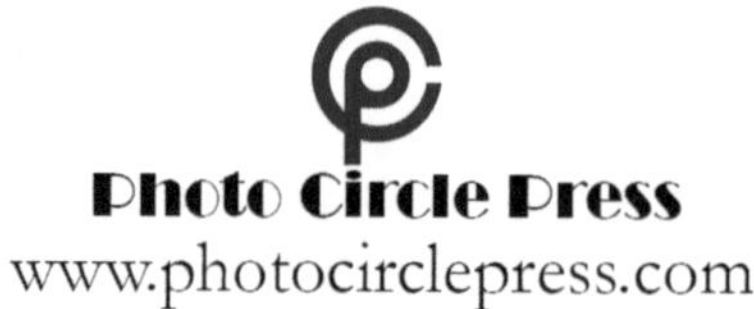

Photo Circle Press
www.photocirclepress.com

Contents

Introductions - 6 - 7

Photographs - 8 - 56

Poems

A Way of Seeing - 9
Sandscape - 11
Questions from Seeing - 13
Tall Tale - 15
The Visual Chord - 17
Juxtaposition - 19
Sight to Sight - 21
Ripple Effect - 23
Seeing the Shadows - 25
A Small Plant's Valediction - 27
La Vie en Rose - 29
Oneironaut - 31
Wonder - 33
Reversal - 35
The Jazz Musicians's Last Show - 37
Celebration - 39
Jazz Pop - 41
B. B. King - 43
Pete Fountain - 45
JazzFest - 47
Waiting - 49
Eyes - 51
Being in the Moment - 53
Life Cycles - 55
To Lou - 57

Poet & Photographer Bios - 58 - 59

Acknowledgements - 61

Jianqing Zheng

I was fascinated with Leo's black-and-white dune photographs when I reviewed Duet, a collection of photos and poems by Leo and his wife Liz. Later, I had the chance to review Leo's photo book, Chasing Shadows, a collection of dune photographs. Leo's photographs present facets of the beauty of dunes that are hard to resist when their visual charms fascinate a viewer like me. The composition of his photos exhibits beautiful shapes made effective by light and shadow with a tension of fluidity and tranquility of the dunes that inspire ekphrastic writing. That's why I started cultivating an artistic imagination in my poetry writing after his dune photographs.

After reviewing all his eight photograph books about society, horse races, children, jazz funerals, flowers, and the life of framed ducks, I feel I have better understood Leo's artistic vision before I find a form to present it through poetry. Often, I would dwell upon the form or try different ways. For example, "Jazz Pop" is a shape poem using the form to suggest the shape of the Coke bottle in Leo's JazzFest photograph and the thin, long lines suggest the jazz funeral procession or second line parade. Several prose poems concluded with haiku indicate the need for narration or monologue, as in "Life Cycles" or "Tall Tale." The combination of prose and haiku juxtaposes two views that complement each other while standing on their own independently. Technically, the use of apostrophe establishes the immediacy of friendship, as in "To Lou."

Poetic ekphrasis engages a communication between imagination and creativity and helps me focus on things, not ideas. Ekphrastic writing is not a retelling of what we see in artworks; it concerns an interaction of the senses, a creation from the original art. Now and then I send my poems to Leo for feedback or chat with him about his photos to seek a view beyond a photo. Over the past few years, I have written twenty-five poems collected in this book. Since ekphrastic poetry is a reinterpretation that experiments with imagination, language, and synesthesia in its creative process, I hope the poems in this duet are a good company to Leo's photographs.

Leo Touchet

My photography career began in 1965 after studying works of photographers like Henri Cartier-Bresson, Eugene Smith, Dorthea Lange, Gordon Parks, Elliott Erwitt, David Seymour and others in the archives of the Museum of Modern Art in New York City. At that time, the archives at MOMA were open to the public. Since then, as a photojournalist and photographer, I've worked for many publications around the world producing photographs for books, magazines, newspapers and advertising.

My wife Elzabeth "Liz" Burk, a psychologist and poet, asked me to accompany her to a poetry reading where she and several other poets were planning to read ekphrastic poems. That word sounded more like a rare tropical disease rather than a poem that responds to a work of art. I was impressed with how the poets were able to write poems inspired by other visual art forms. The poets read poems which were inspired by paintings, and paintings were exhibited which were inspired by poems. That experience motivated us to publish DUET, a joint book of her ekphrastic poems written to a selection on my photographs. Later, Liz was asked to write an essay on Jianqing's poetry to appear in a journal about Mississippi Delta poets. She had never been to northern Mississippi, so I suggested a first-hand view of the Delta.

We drove up the Mississippi River Delta from Louisiana to Northern Mississippi. We met Jianqing for the first time in Clarksdale, Mississippi. I was familiar with Liz's poetry, but not being a poet myself, I sat back and listened to them discussing poetry and their connections in the poetry world. I then found out that Jianqing was interested in photography. Since then, we have had many meetings over lunch with fried green tomatoes and other good foods at the Crystal Grill Cafe in nearby Greenwood, Mississippi.

Jianqing was fascinated with my photos of sand dunes and later reviewed my book Chasing Shadows. He later traveled West to see the dunes himself. After his trip, he mentioned the difficulty of photographing the dunes. He realized that the shadows disappeared as the sun rose above the horizon. The only times you can actually photograph the dunes is during the first and last half hours of the day when the sun is low and causing shadows.

We've visited Jianqing several time over the last few years. On our last trip through Greenwood, Jianqing suggested a book of his work with my photos. I immediately agreed to publish this book. He selected the photographs and wrote the poetry which accompanied my photographs.

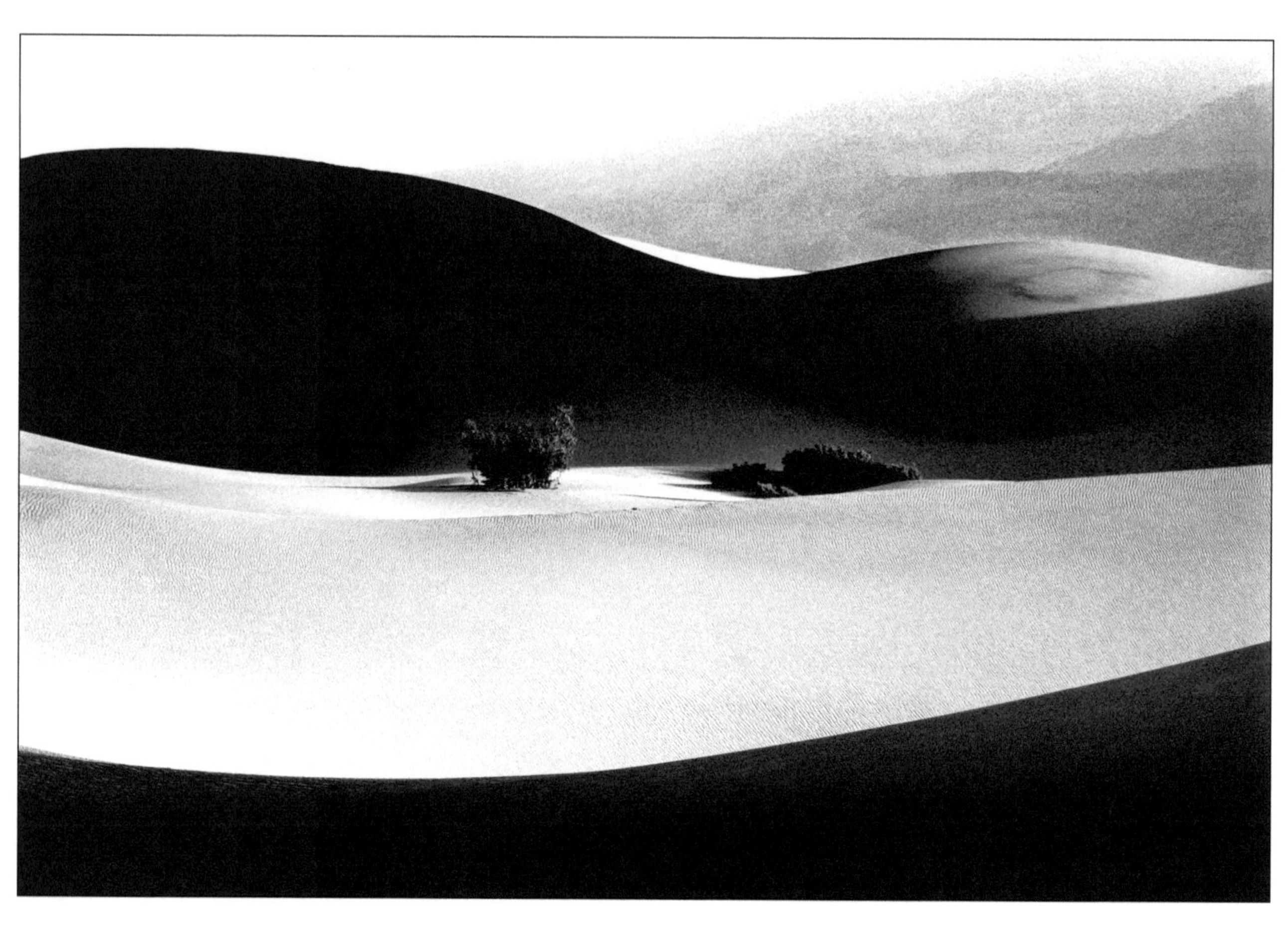

Mesquite Flats Sand Dunes
Death Valley Nartional Park, California 1994

A Way of Seeing

Those
sand
dunes

(tension
of time
and space

touch
of light
and shade

shape
of solitude
and company)

look
serene
and jumpy

under
sun
and moon

as if
ready
to swing

dance
in swirling
wind

each
a mass
of harmony

and
dissonance
between

being
and
nonbeing

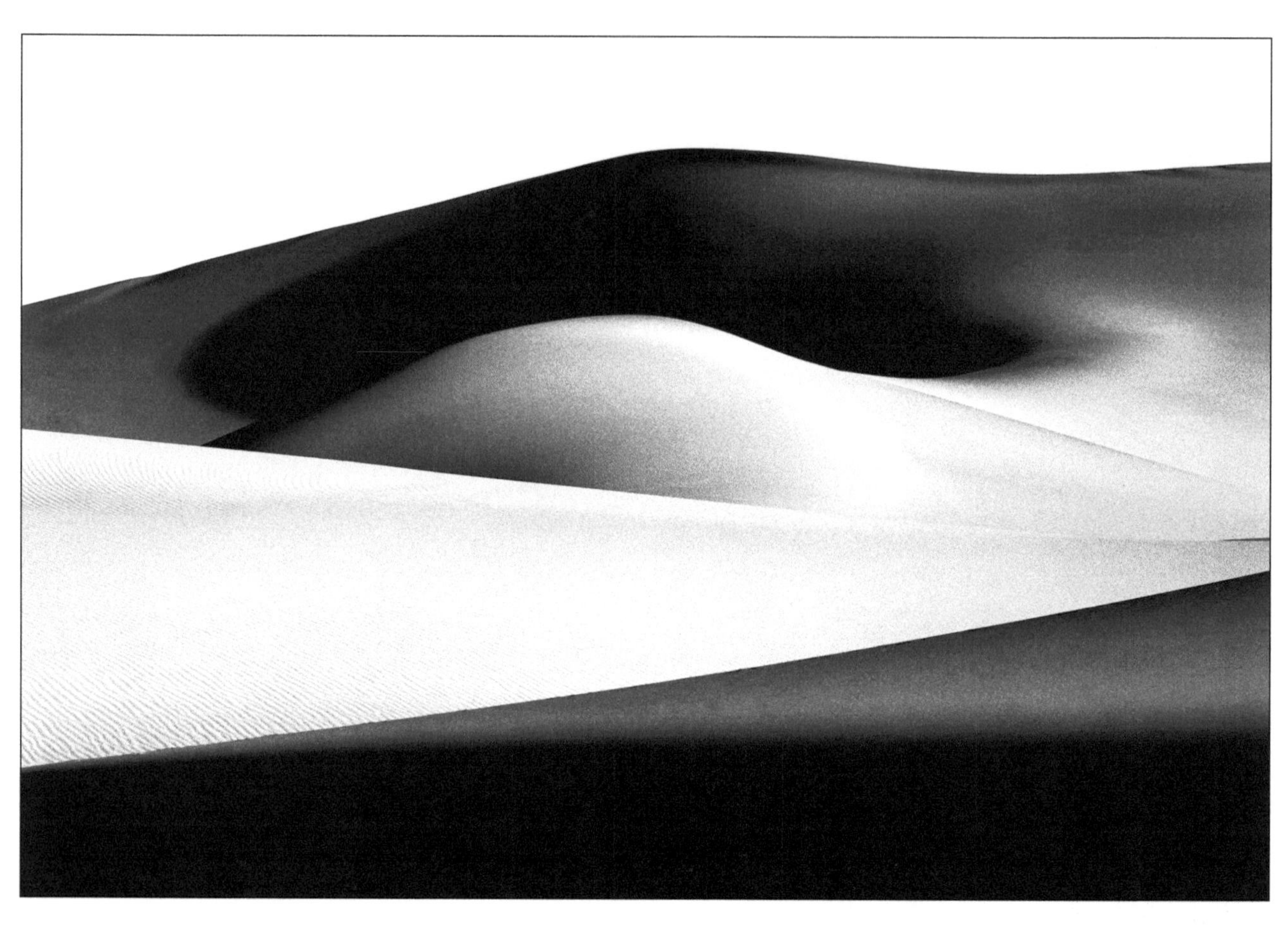

Mesquite Flats Sand Dunes
Death Valley Nartional Park, California 1994

Sandscape

The dunes
are curving,
rounding,
or slanting
into magic
shapes
of shadow
and light
to form
a live view
of abstract art:
a sleeping
beauty
in stillness
and motion
making you
utter
Eureka
upon seeing her.

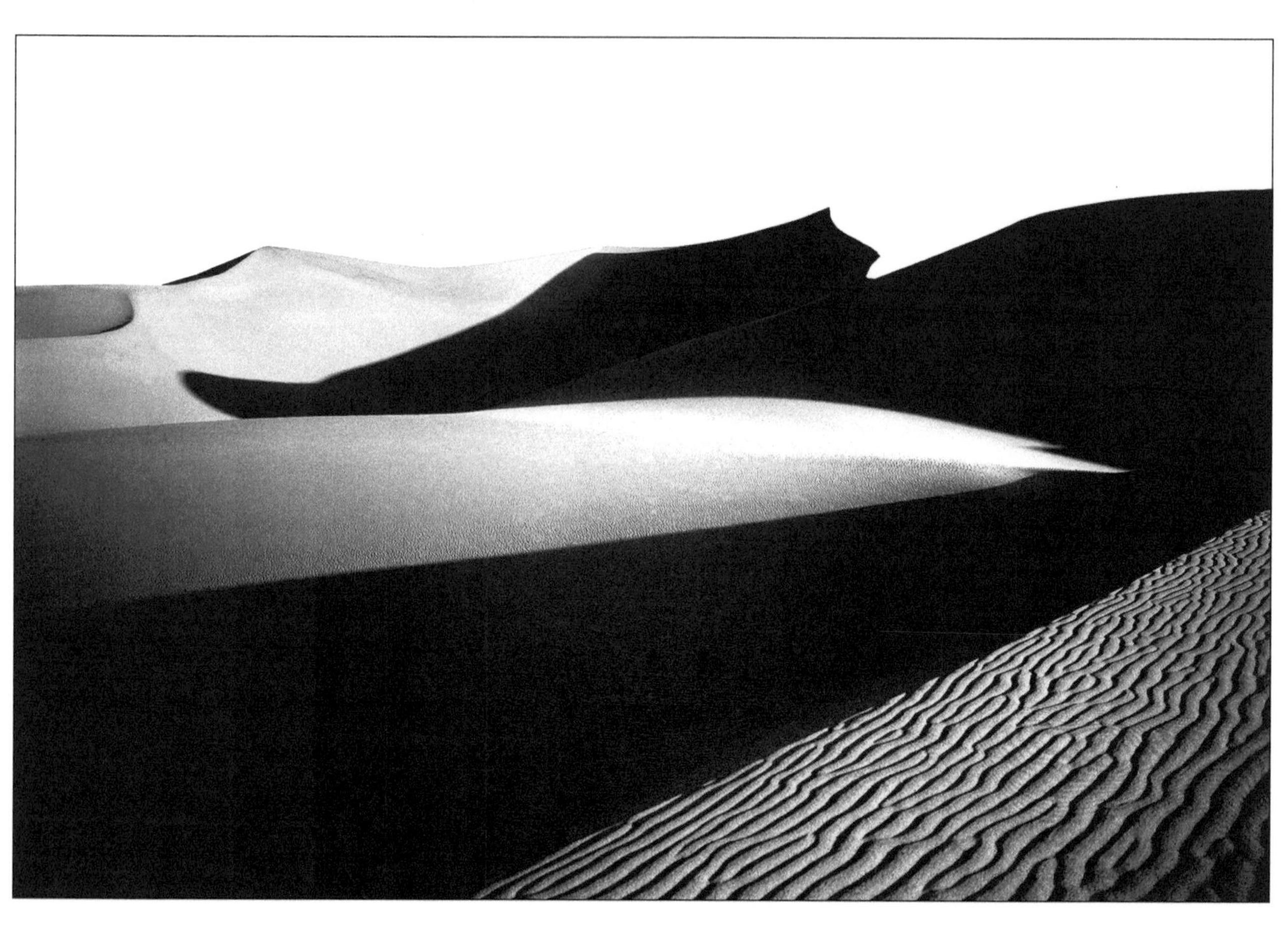

Mesquite Flats Sand Dunes
Death Valley Nartional Park, California 1996

Questions from Seeing

The background shadow looks like
a mummy of an Egyptian pharaoh

and the foreground sand ripples like
a pyramid labyrinth in darkness.

If ancient burial means eternal peace,
why should it be disturbed?

But after the buried is unearthed
for research or exhibition, what is seen

after a mummy is unwrapped cautiously?
An object for preservation study or

a body as dry as a dead Joshua tree?
As you walk near a mummy case

in the museum, do you shudder
at those big, painted, and staring eyes?

Who has a stronger desire to see?
A researcher, a museumgoer, or

the dry mummy who may be able
to silently watch us doing whatnot?

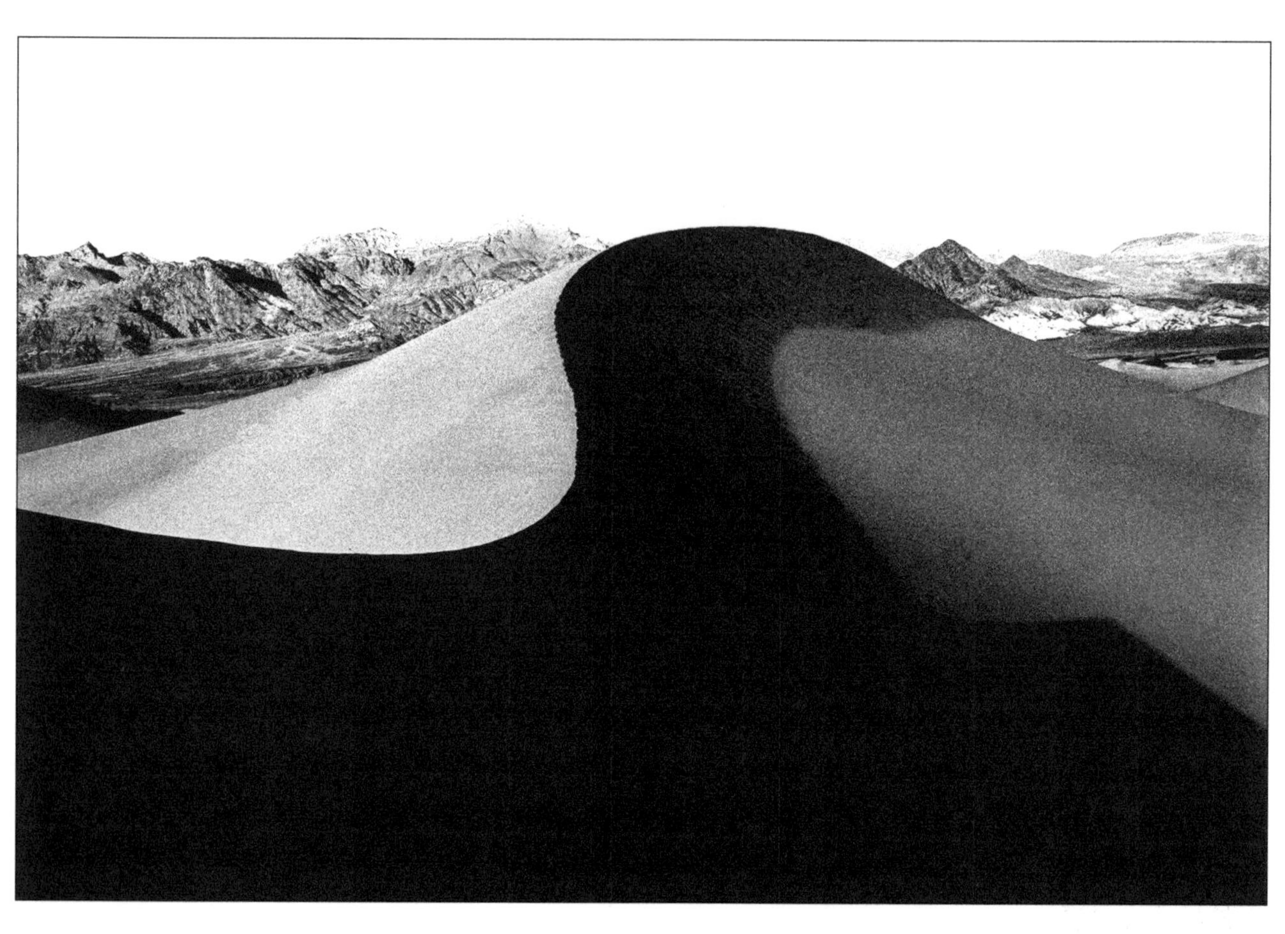

Mesquite Flats Sand Dunes
Death Valley Nartional Park, California 1994

Tall Tale

One evening in Death Valley I wandered on dunes to look for the ideal chiaroscuro to grab a view of beauty. I like to shoot dunes. At the right moment of light and shade, they look like reclining women full of the charm of nature. While I was mindful of catching beauty, a loud sound sharp as a blade suddenly cut through the sky and echoed in all directions. It gave me the creeps. I looked up. A giant blackbird flapped its wings overhead. I stared hard at it, fearing it would swoop down on me. It did swoop down, not on me but farther away down on a lee side. A heavy thump stirred up sand dust into an ominous mushroom cloud expanding in the sky. I tramped to the crash site and found the bird motionless, its wide wings spreading like a museum specimen. Later, when I showed my photographs to some ornithologists, they all felt thrilled. It was a thunderbird that could fly nonstop for ninety thousand miles. It was extinct before humans learned to walk on Earth. Now it returns. Believe it or not, this was the biggest discovery in the last 100 years.

camping night
crickets chirp words
known to stars

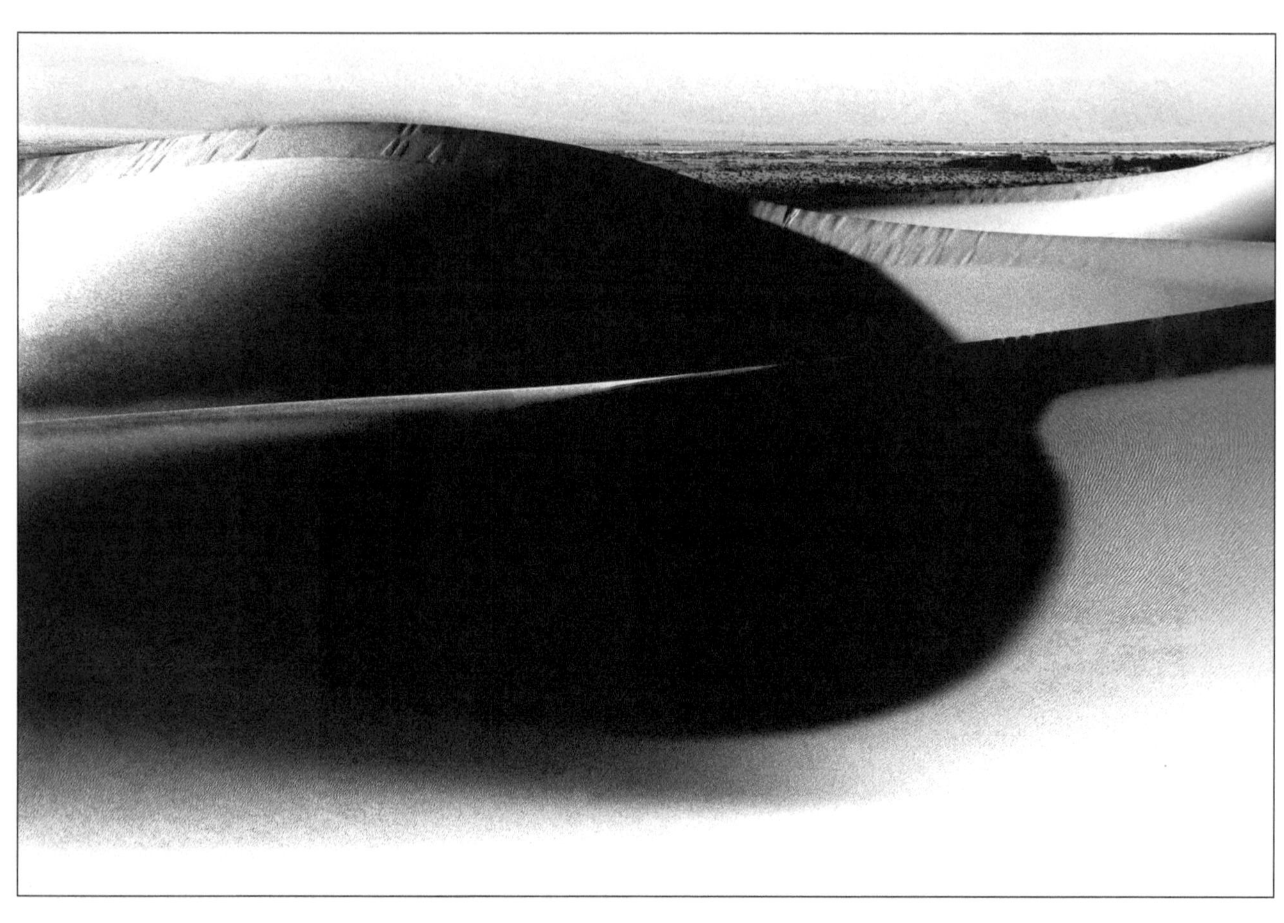

Mesquite Flats Sand Dunes
Death Valley Nartional Park, California 1996

The Visual Chord

The beguiling light and shade form variant images out of dunes to allure you to grab pictures and exclaim delightful surprises. When light slides away and you are on your way to the tent, shade expands inch by inch into an oblong image unexpected and awesome again to the eye:

> stranded on beach
> a humpback whale
> in desperate silence

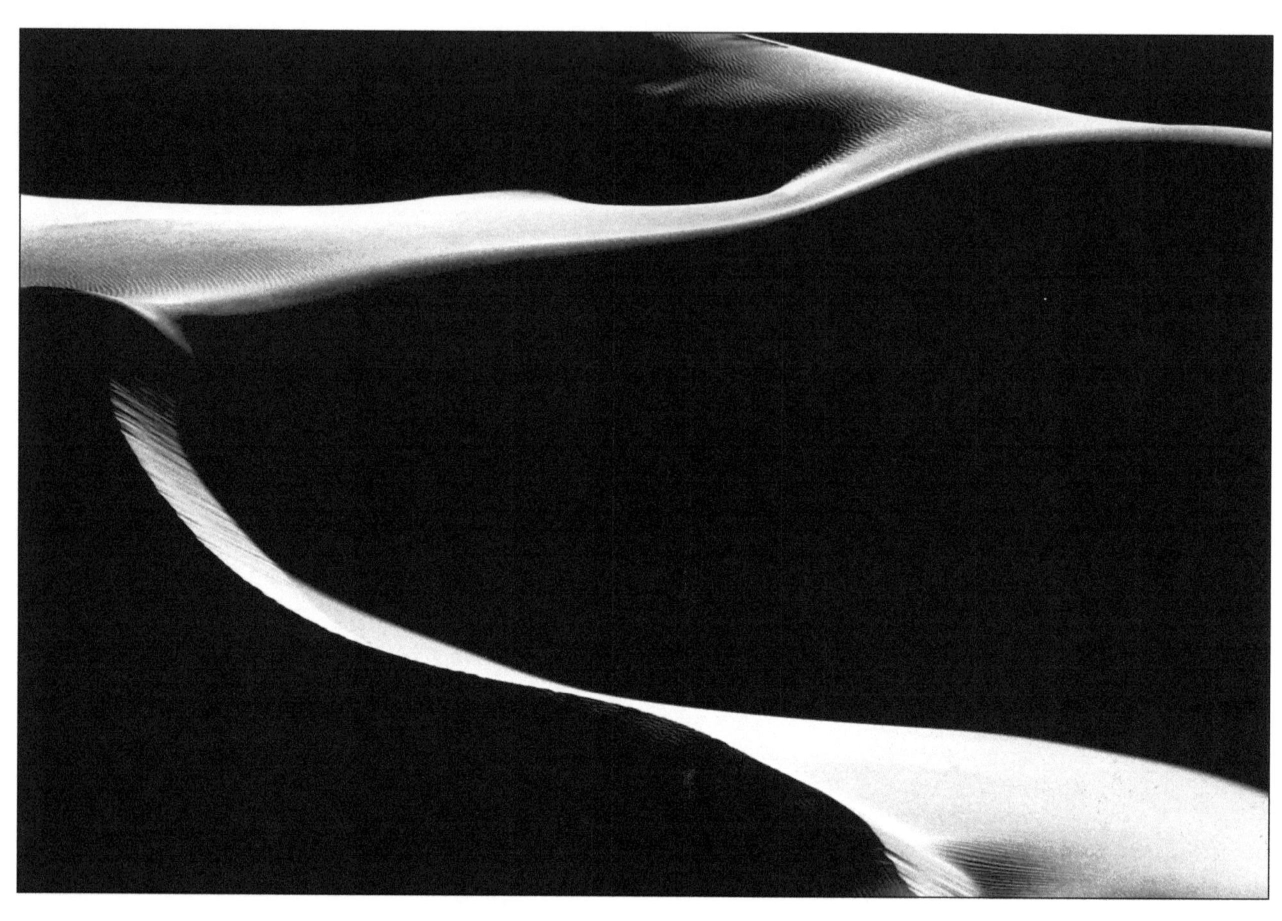

Eureka Valley Dunes
Death Valley Nartional Park, California 1996

Juxtaposition

These petroglyphs
deserve a second look

about expressions
conveyed through images:

a whooping crane
flapping its wide wings,

a reclining body
luring light and shade

to shape a view
of beauty, a ski trail

down the mountain,
or something too simple

for meaning but
strikes the eye

for a response
of oohs and aahs

that ski down
into silent awe of dunes.

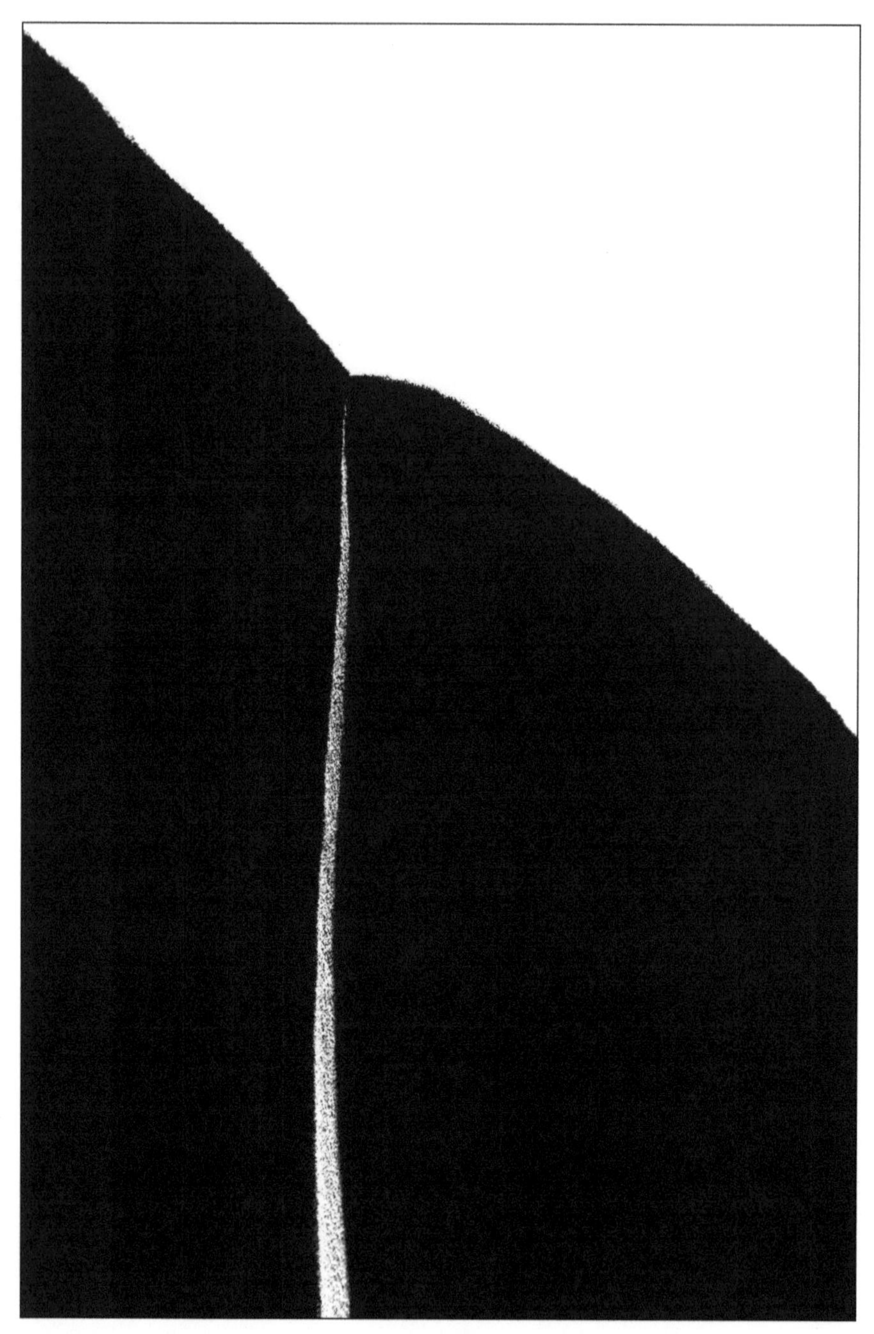

Mesquite Flats Sand Dunes
Death Valley Nartional Park, California 1996

Sight to Sight

As a photographer, Leo thinks an image is worth a thousand words. A dune photograph taken in Death Valley best presents his belief. The simplicity of its composition of light and shade is an invitation for imagination. The top right is a triangle of white space for the sky. It takes one-third of the composition and shifts the focus to two-thirds of the dark dune striking the eye. The dark line tipping from the top left makes the dark dune like a shoulder.

afterglow
her curving line
slants on sand

The compelling part is a white line dangling downright from the top of the dark dune—a finishing touch that perfects the composition for an aesthetic taste. This white line, which may be a ridge trail, is the key to imagination. Is it a line-of-sky waterfall seen in the mountains, or a noodle strap of a dress worn to a gala? Leo is sharp to catch the feminine beauty of dunes, so it must be a strap dangling to attract the eye.

desert moon
undressing for bath
by the lake

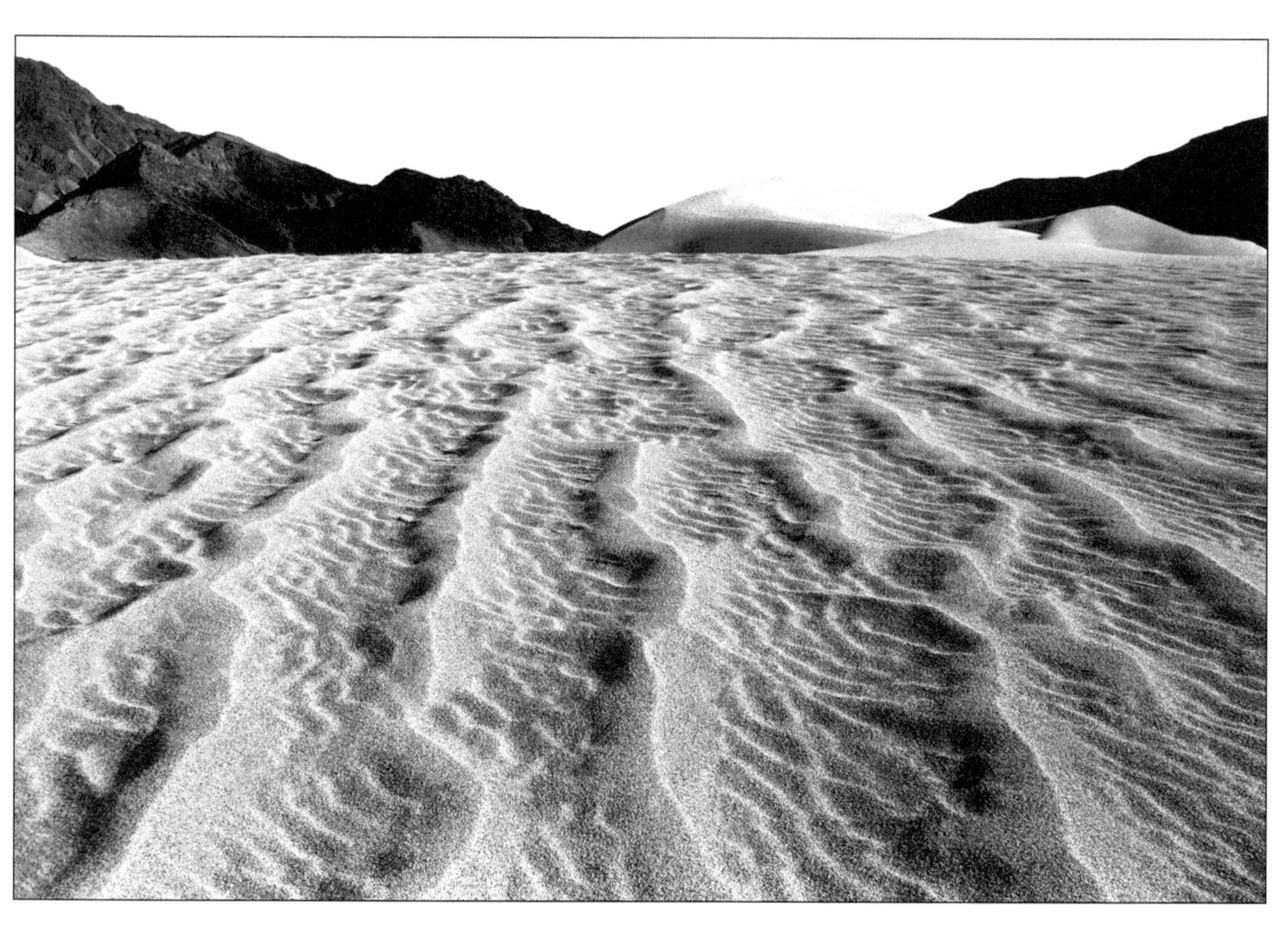

Mesquite Flats Sand Dunes
Death Valley Nartional Park, California 1996

Ripple Effect

Wind blows sand to bounce into a natural painting of lake ripples pushing on and on into more ripples stretching out of sight.

> seeing
> two swans'
> lake ballet
> we start to pace
> arm in arm

This view charming the eye may not charm the mind in real life. When inflation causes low employment and high prices of food and services, its ripple effect casts a collective shadow out of sight.

> pillow talk
> about delayed retirement
> delays sleep

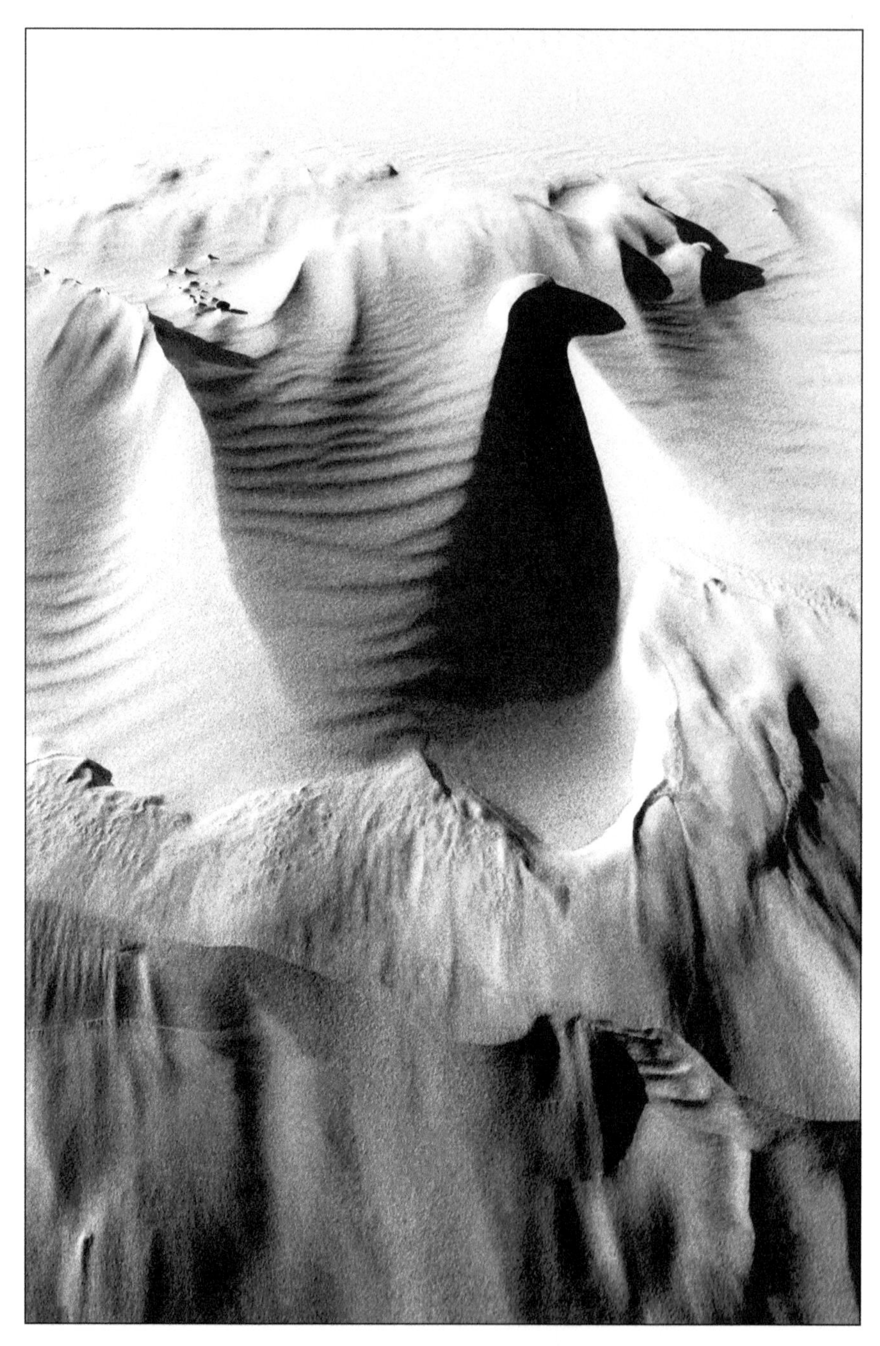

Monahans Sand Hills Dunes
Monahans Sand Hills State Park, Texas 1994

Seeing the Shadows

Now a seagull
drifting on ripples,

now an origami
with folded wings,

now an iceberg
collapsing into sea,

now nothing
but hulking dunes

resembling
burial mounds,

now shadows
changing shapes

with light sliding
across sands—

a long reptile
wriggling into

a silhouette
against seeing.

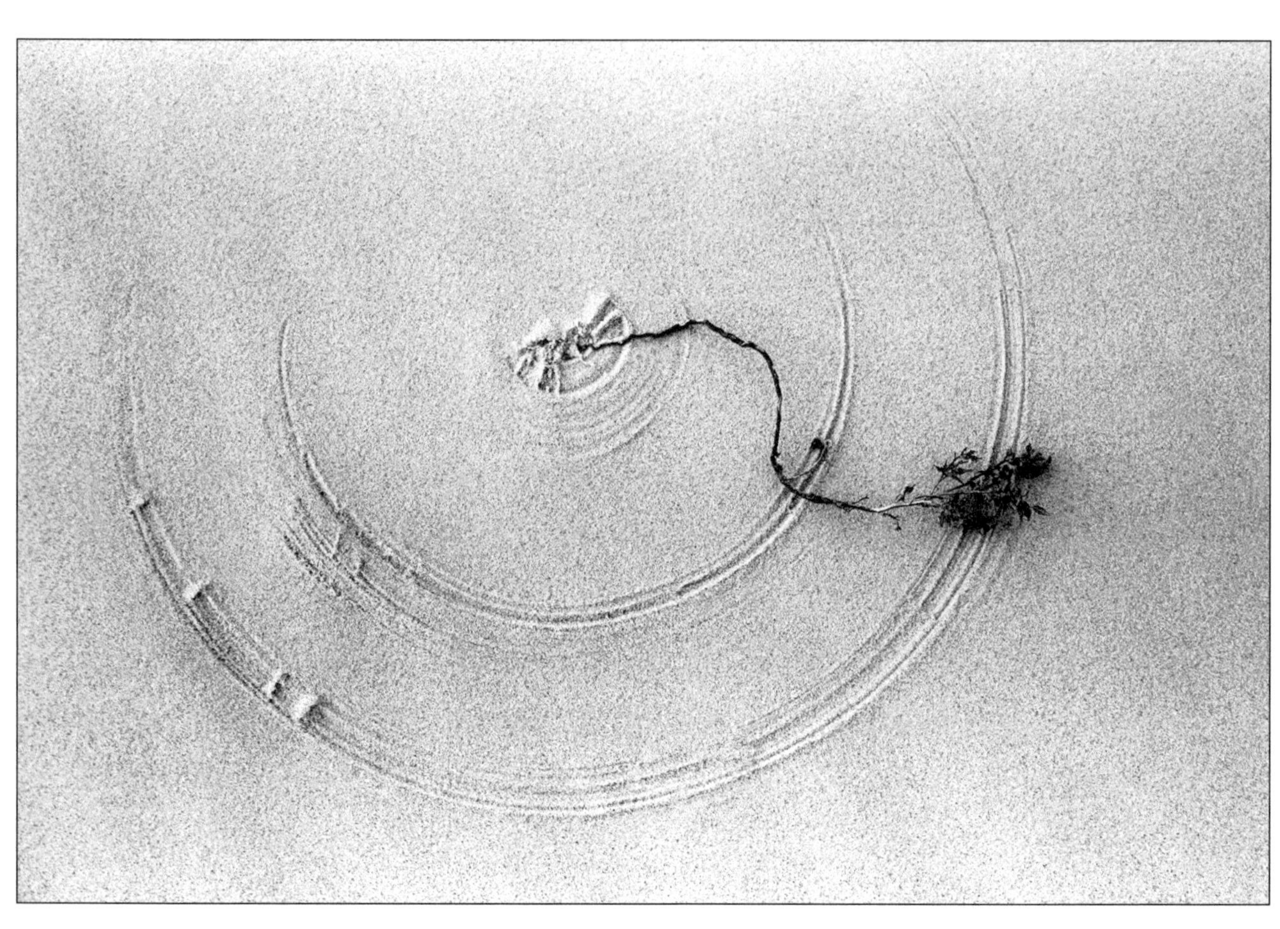

Monahans Sand Hills Dunes
Monahans Sand Hills State Park, Monohans, Texas 1994

A Small Plant's Valediction

Dear Sand, don't creep into sadness. I won't leave you for good no matter how hot you grow under the burning sun because I am an hour hand attached to your shaft. I want to stretch my roots to make a circle to perfect my desert life. To survive, I must twist my growth to avoid being buried by you. Even if wind may shove your grains into a mound over me, my half circle already shows my death wish for a round-the-world trip before I dry into a walking stick.

second coming
a touch of green
out of nowhere

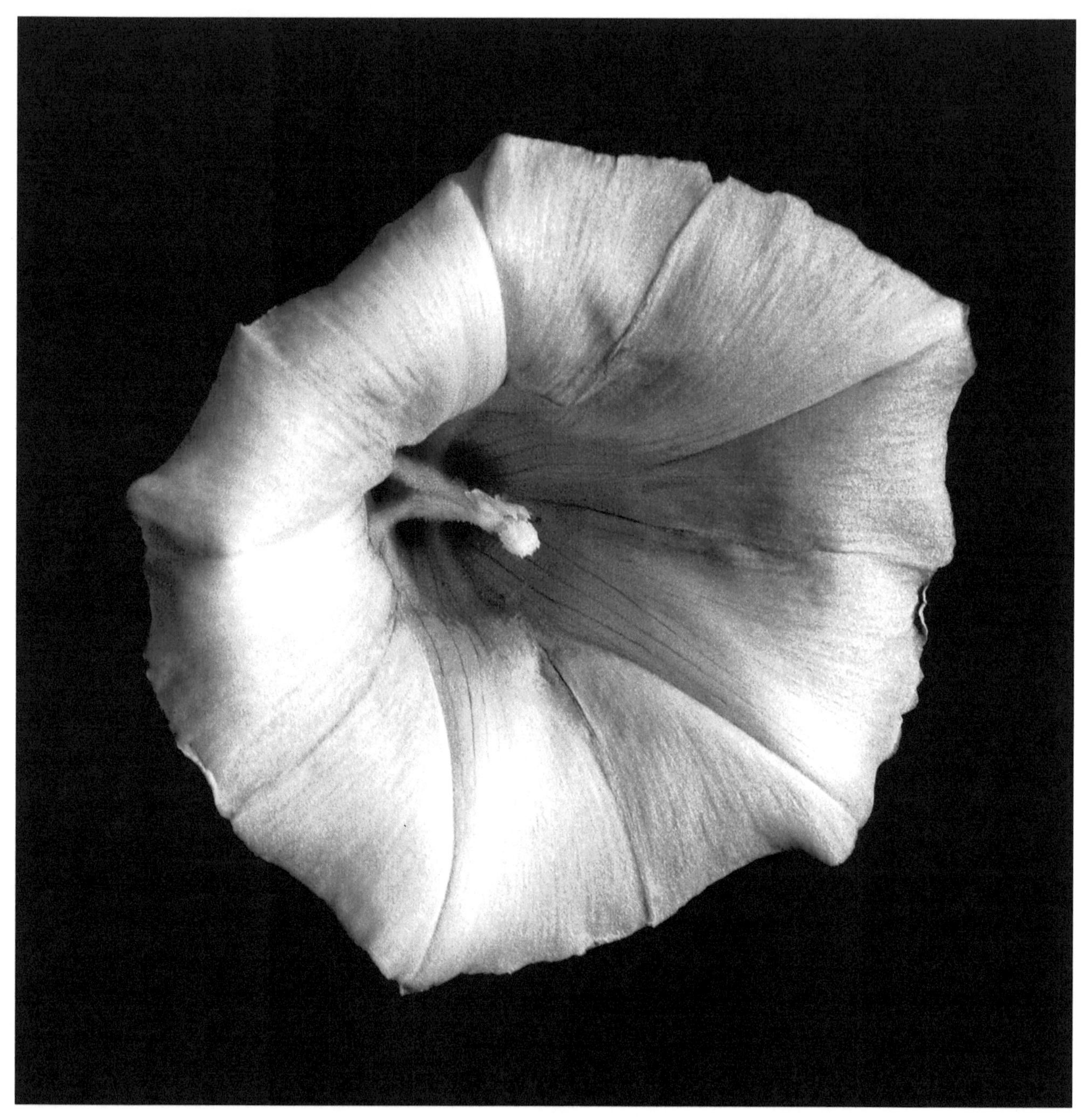

Flower
New Orleans, Louisiana 2005

La Vie en Rose

Armstrong's song
blooms through
a gramophone trumpet
found at Goodwill—

Good old days
hold me close
and hold me fast
and beg me

not to sigh
and say goodbye
and go to a world apart

because life will
always be La vie en rose
as beautiful as a dream.

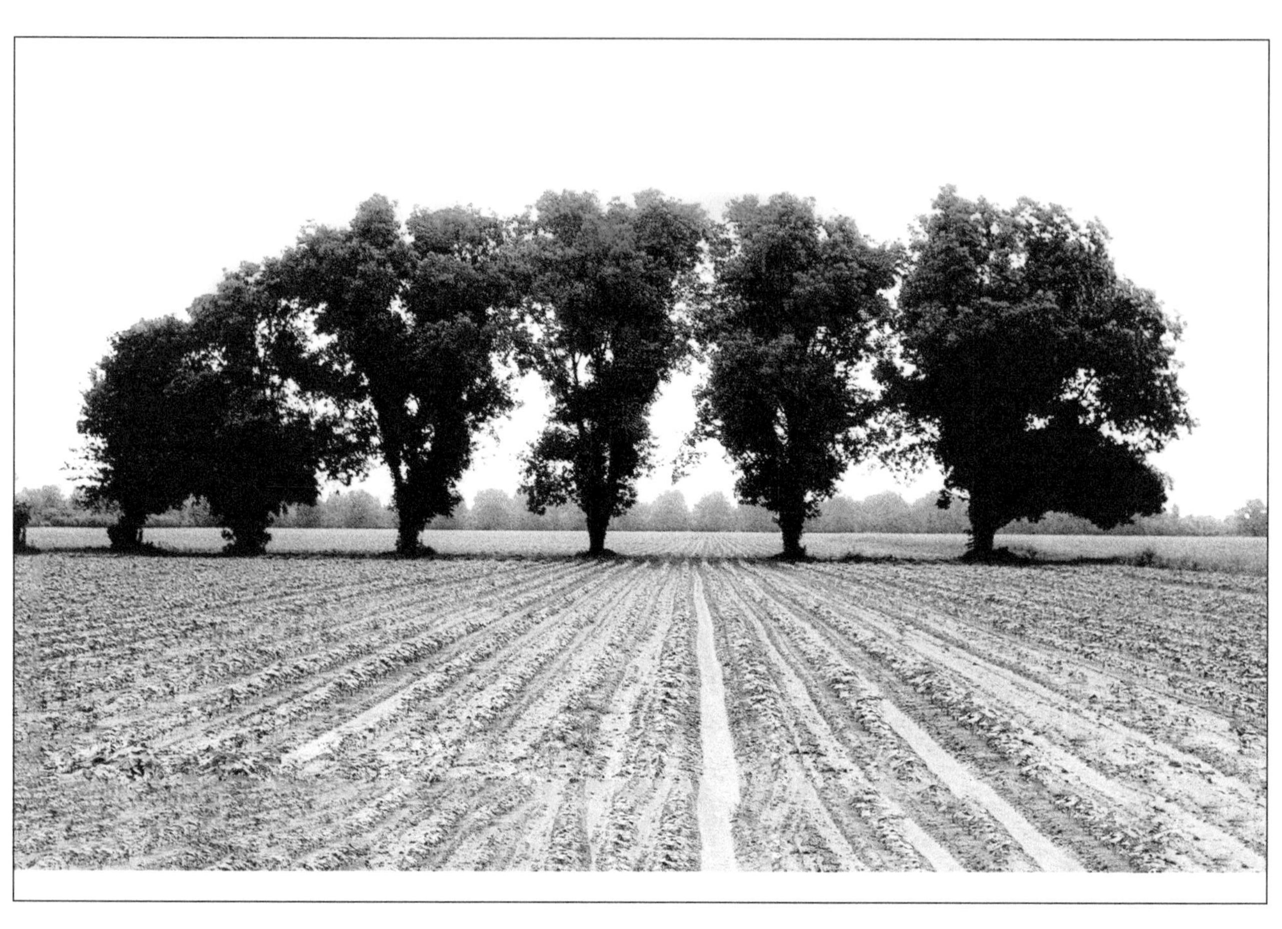

SUGAR CANE FIELD AF TER HARVEST
VERMILION PARISH, LOUISIANA 1991

Oneironaut

Wow, those uniform ridges line like dwarf droids at attention for military review. Six trees, each like a General Pong Krell with a solemn look, stand in a row, tall and straight, a posture showing might and main. Now wind blows the bugle. The formation starts to mark time and clouds kick hooves. Droids salute and goose-step in synchrony until their battle cry rolls into afterglow.

field song row after row of sugarcanes

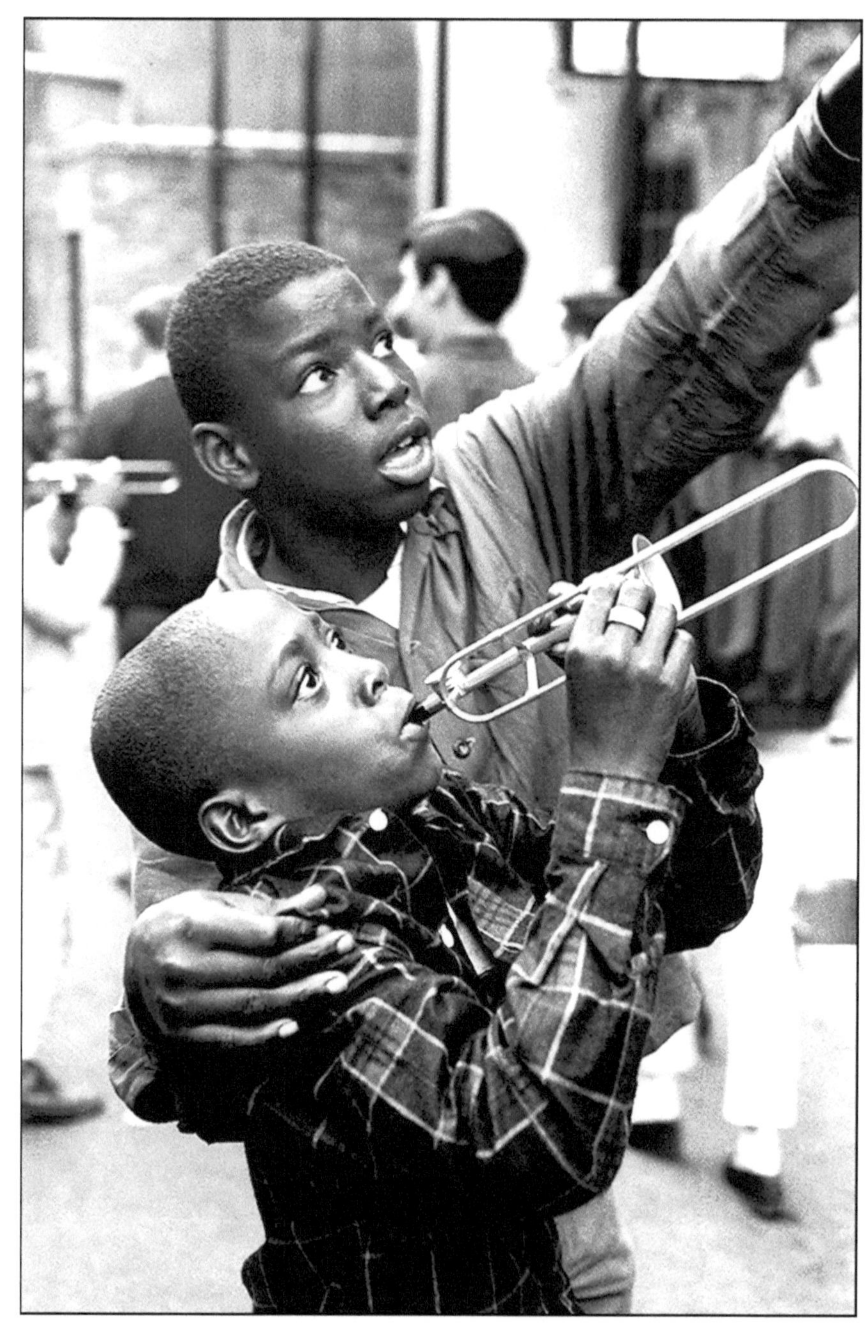

Bourbon Street in the French Quarter
New Orleans, Louisiana 1968

Wonder

Bourbon Street,
a smaller boy
playing a small
trumpet looks up,

a taller boy pats
the small one
on the shoulder,

saying with his
other hand pointing
to the direction:

“Bro, it’s there.”
Their wide eyes
explore something
so new to them…

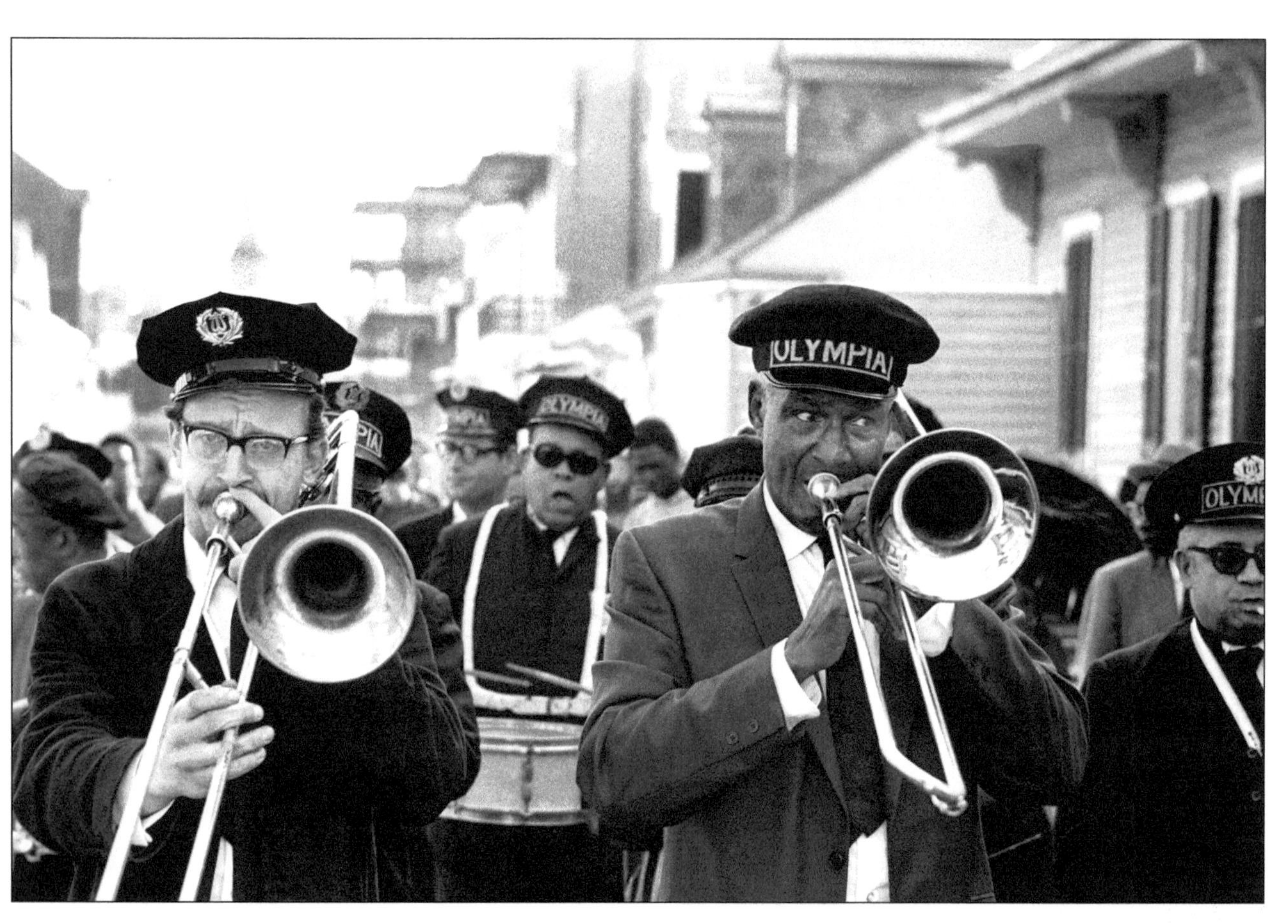

Musicians in a Jazz Funeral Processionl
New Orleans, Louisiana 1969

Reversal

After the jazz procession
swings to the tomb

the second line
begins with a whining

clarinet and drums
to blow beat bebop boom

into a cheerful celebration
so long so long

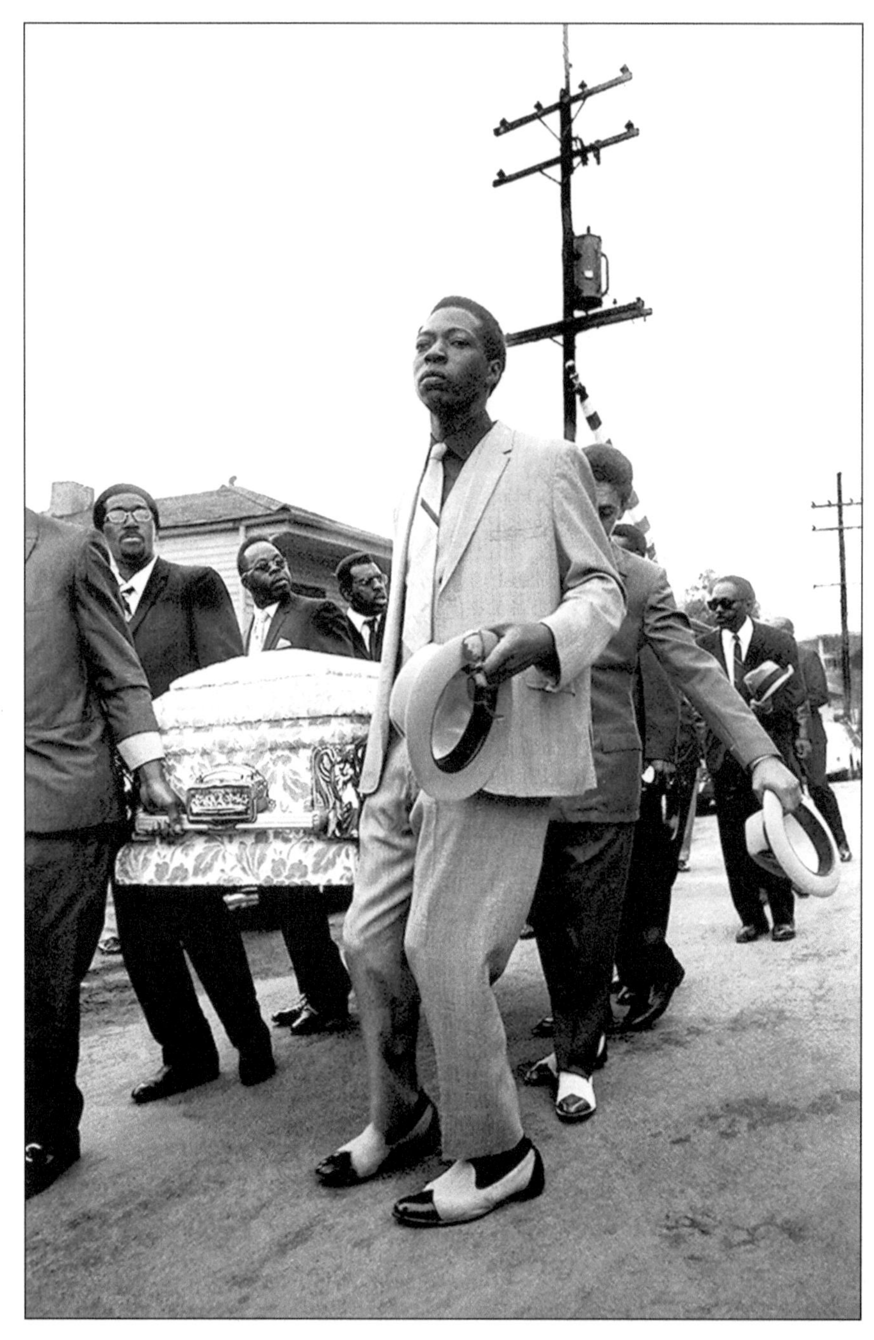

Pallbearers at Leon "Nooney Boy" Shelly's Jazz Funeral
New Orleans, Louisiana 1969

The Jazz Musician's Last Show

Down
the
street

tears
swing
into
moans
of
mourners

wind
swings
into
somber
beats
of
jazz
band

and
casket
swings
to
give
the
last
show
of
the
dead
musician

before
laid
to
final
rest

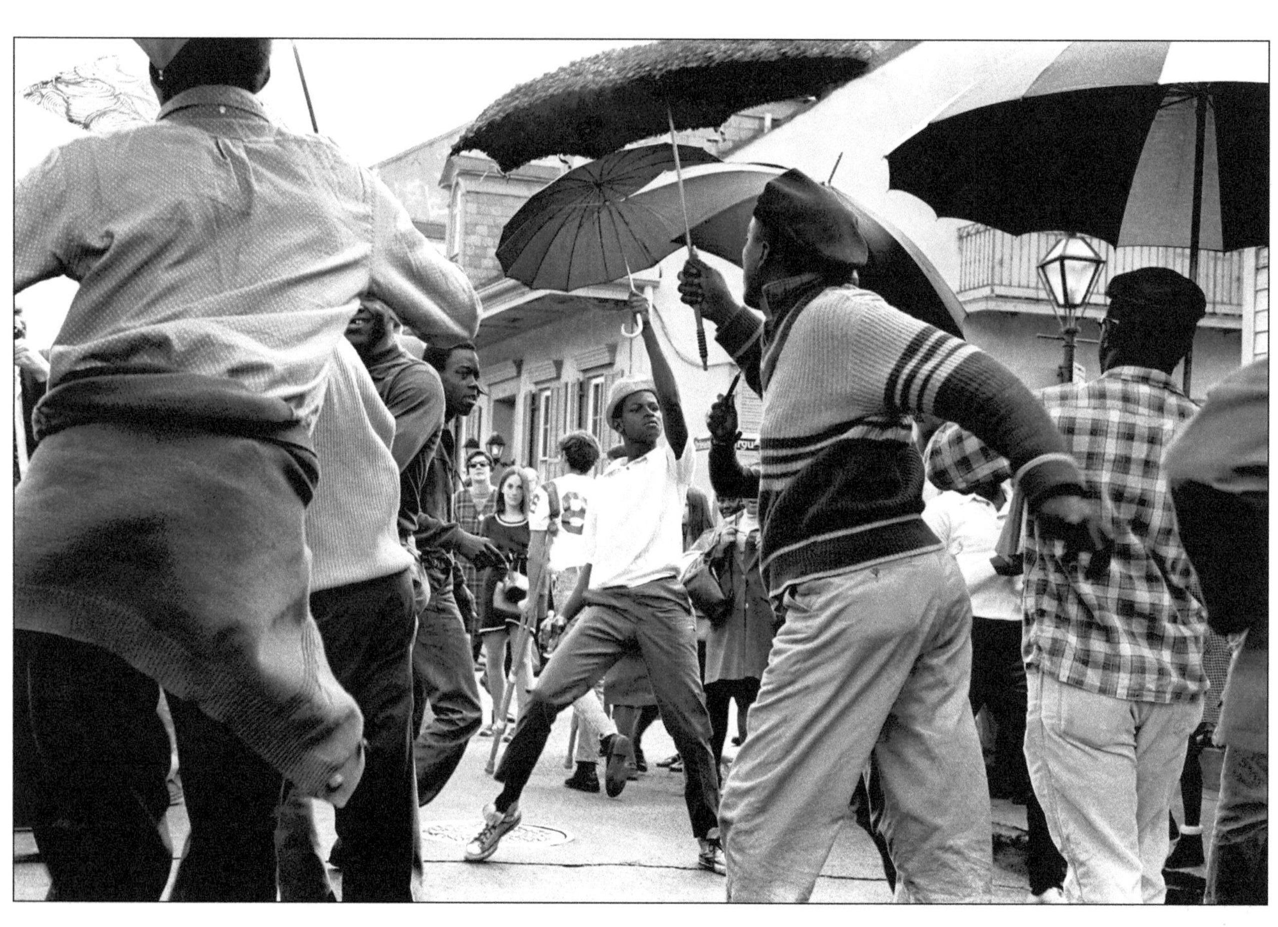

Second Line at Alcide "Slowdrag" Pavageau's Jazz Funeral
New Orleans, Louisiana 1969

Celebration

or

l f
o u
c l

u
m
b
r
e
l
l
a
s

images
of
the Second Line

hip
&
hop

strut
&
booty bounce

rejoicing
the
dead

who's
turning
his back

with
a
smirk

in
the
burial vault

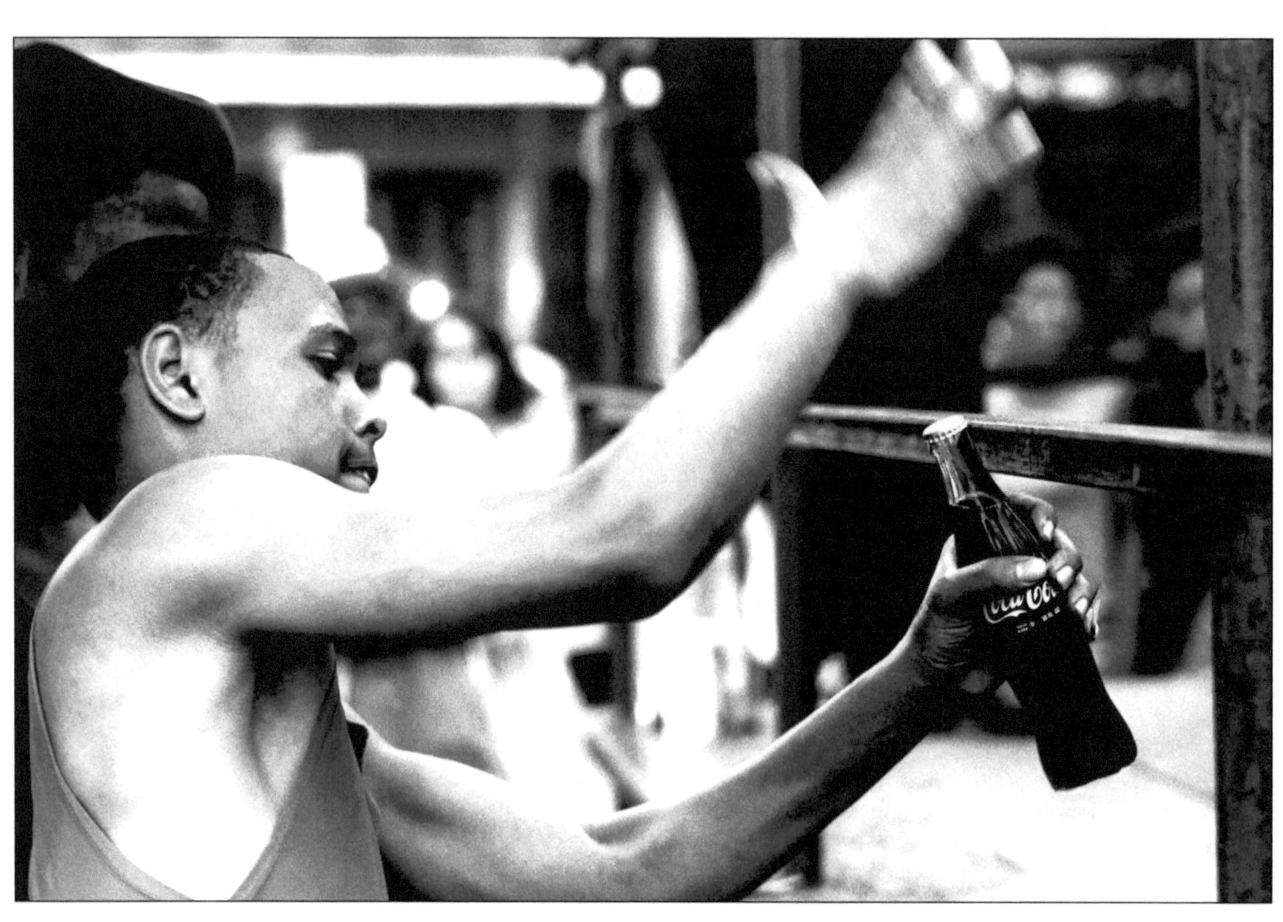

Annual JazzFest in the French Quarter
New Orleans, Louisiana 1969

Jazz Pop

Pop
pop
pop pop
the young
man grips
the coke
bottle in
one hand
places the
crimps on
the edge
of a rung

the
palm
of his
other hand
strikes on
the cap
to pop it
off with
a fizz of
jazz pop
pop pop

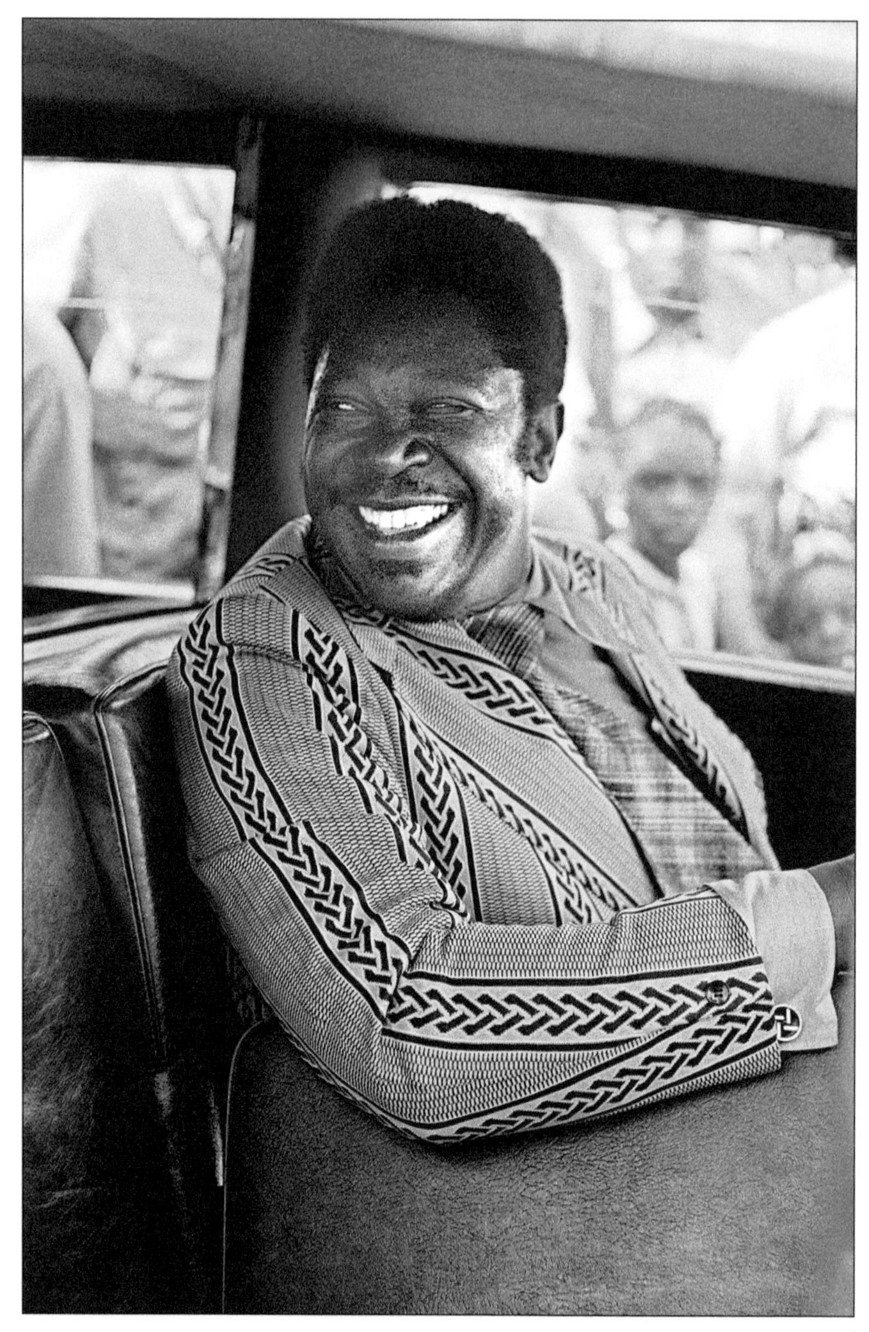

B. B. King at Annual JazzFest
New Orleans, Louisiana 1972

B. B. King

As crowds like sunflowers
surround the hot blues star
sitting gladly inside his car,

King looks around spreading
his broad smile as hot
as the southern sun which

"even a blind man can tell
when he's walkin' in the sun"—
Sunflowers bow with a hail.

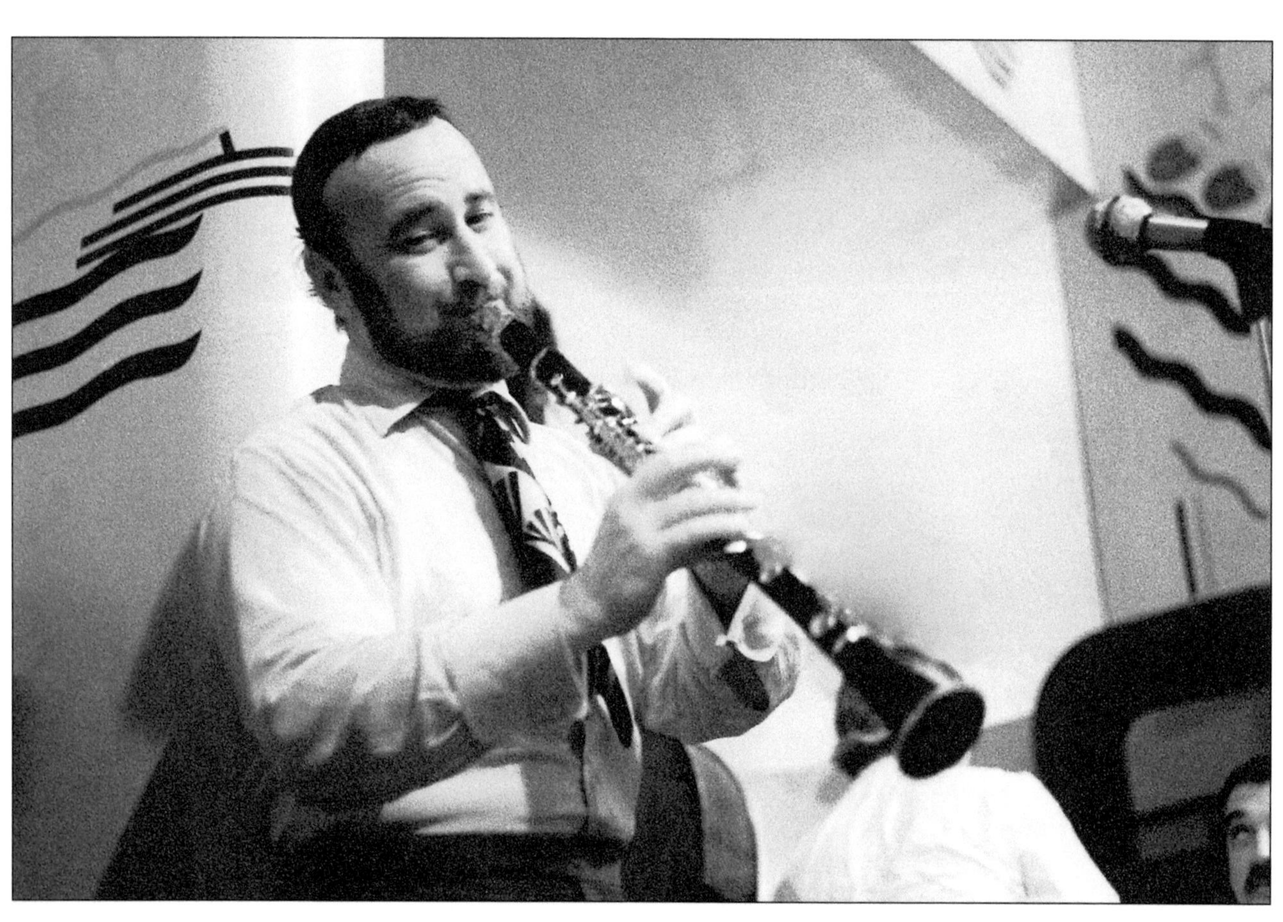

Pete Fountain on Riverboat for Annual JazzFest
New Orleans, Louisiana 1968

Pete Fountain

A riverboat jazz:
the clarinet swings
side to side

to charm the hearts
for a sleepless
night.

Pete's play refreshes
a dreamscape
of a jazz trio:

Fountain's clarinet
Jumbo's trumpet
Fats' piano

erupting into
an ecstasy
along Bourbon Street.

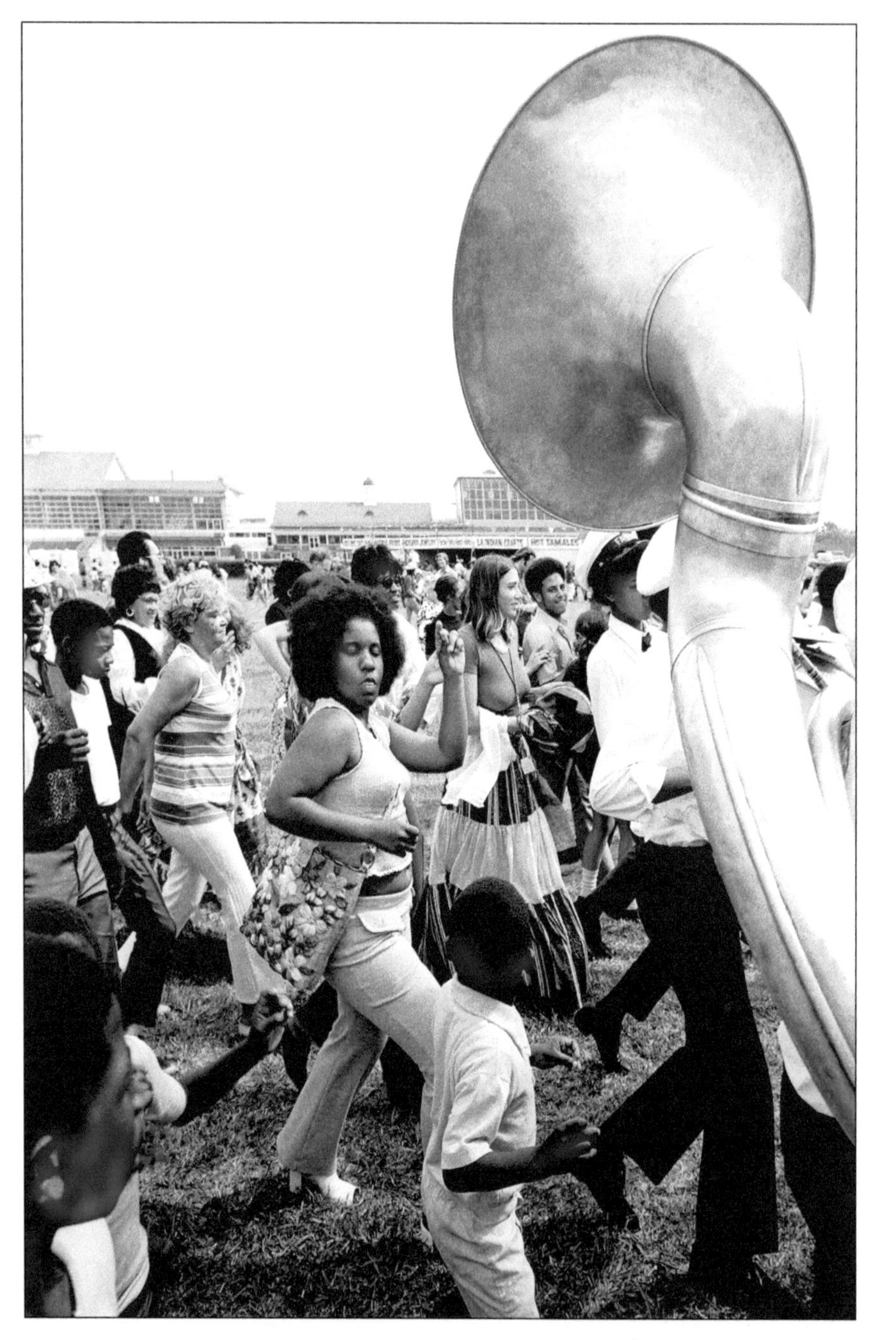

Crowd at Annual JazzFest
New Orleans, Louisiana 1972

JazzFest

Loud tubas blow the crowds
into lapping waves
in the rhythm of jazz.

Excitement shakes
bumps kicks side-steps
into rounds of hollers

surging louder and louder
into a constant flow
of the Mississippi River

to meet the sea
the ocean and everywhere
around the world.

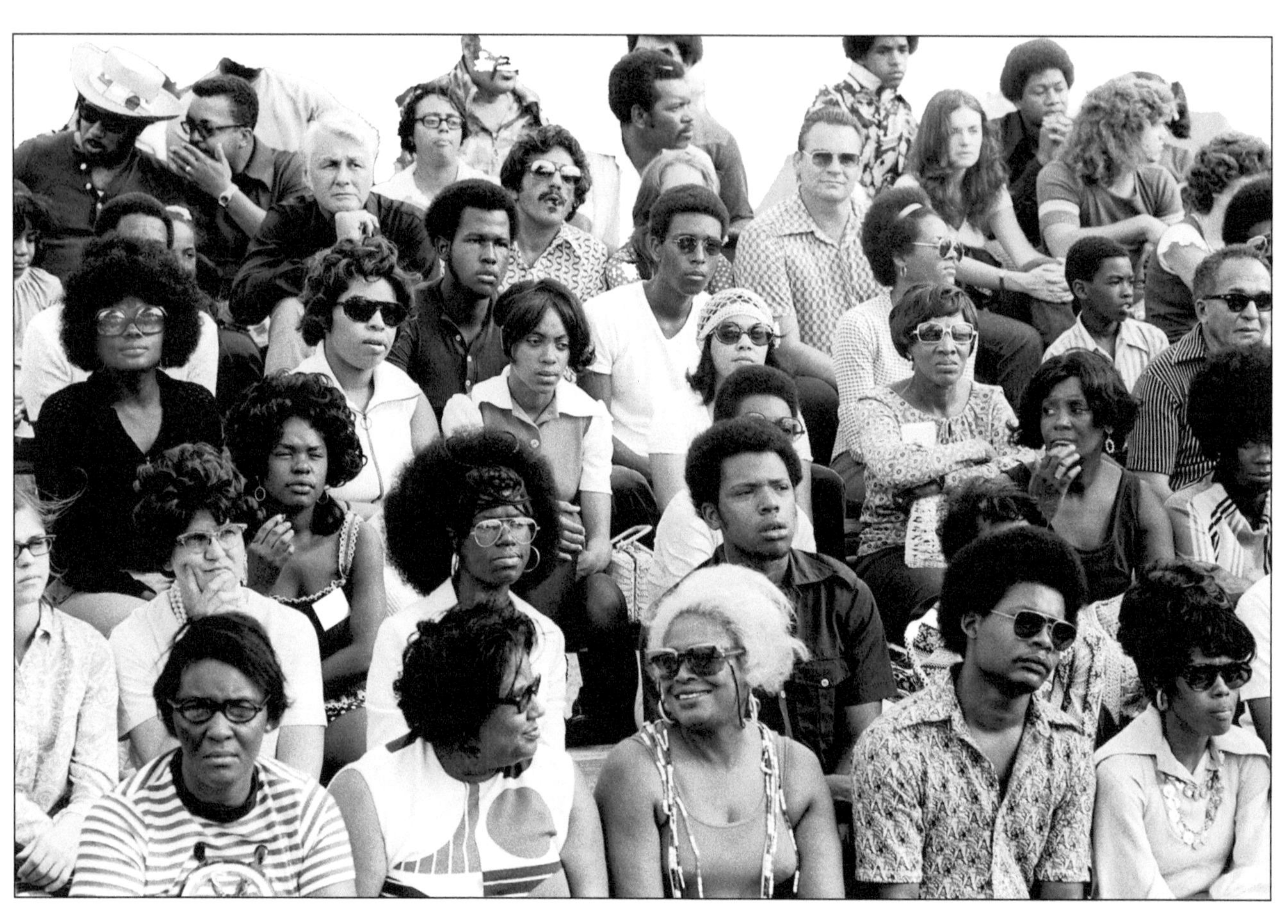

Crowd at Annual JazzFest
New Orleans, Louisiana 1972

Waiting

Rows of audience, black and white,
sit patiently under the April sun.

Two women chat in the front row,
a man covers his mouth with his

left hand to whisper in the back row.
Some wear sunglasses or smiles,

but most show poker faces, as blank
as terracotta figures. Who are they

waiting for? The loud marching band
or top stars like Thelonious Monk,

B. B. King, Sonny Stitt, Art Blakey,
Dizzy Gillespie or Kai Winding?

Suddenly they all look in the direction
where cheers start to surge over.

They get excited. Soon their waiting
will erupt into a volcano to shake

the ground of their bodies
to express their love of jazz.

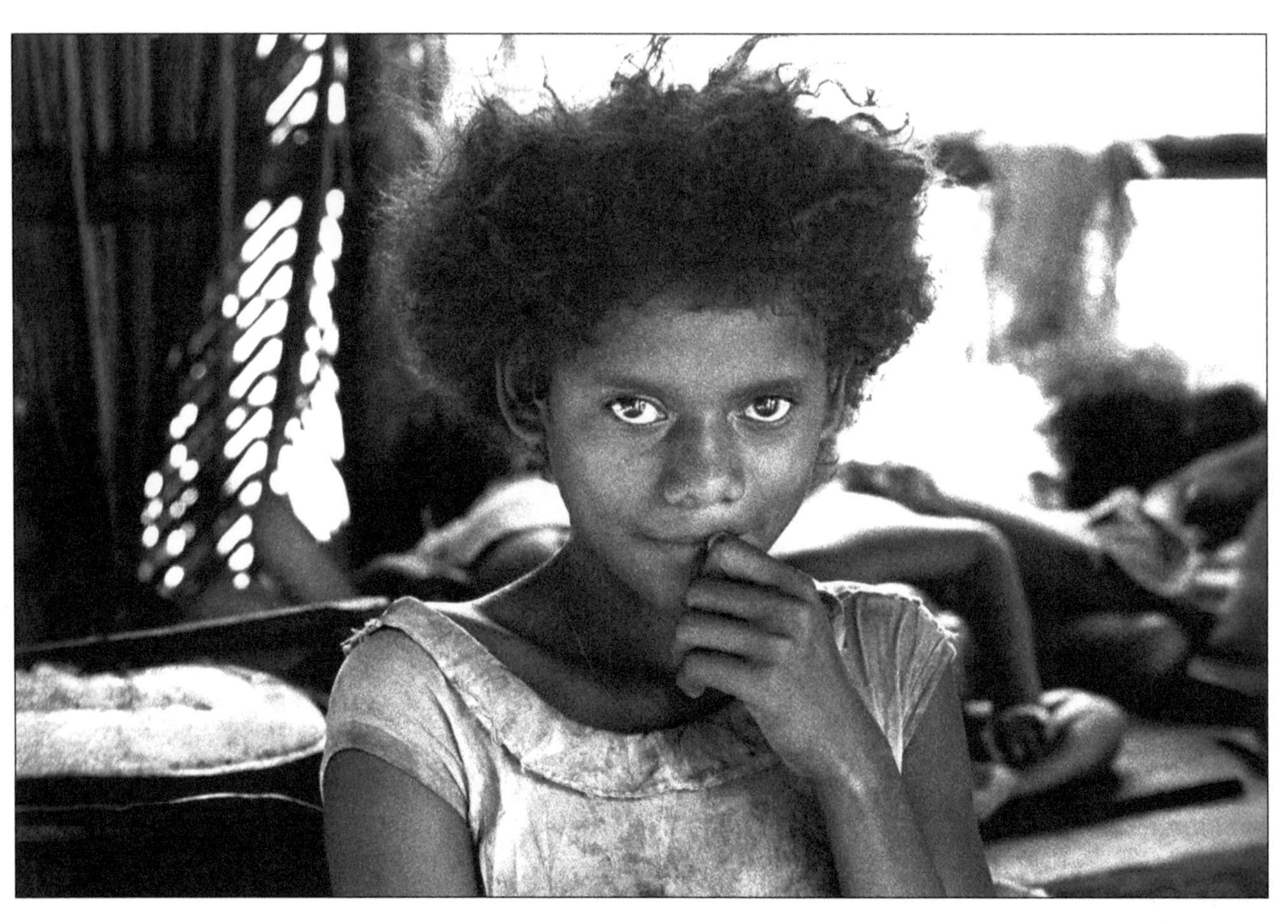

Miskito Indian Girl
Gracias a Dios Department, Honduras 1968

Eyes

What's arresting are the eyes
of a Miskito Indian girl
who stands in a shabby hut

and stares at the camera,
which must intrigue her
curiosity to spark and shine

with an innocent light—
a light that children have
but adults have long lost.

The girl lifts her left hand
to touch her closed mouth
as if to hold the delight

she may utter and her eyes
glitter like a shy smile
budding for this beautiful

moment snapped in one click.

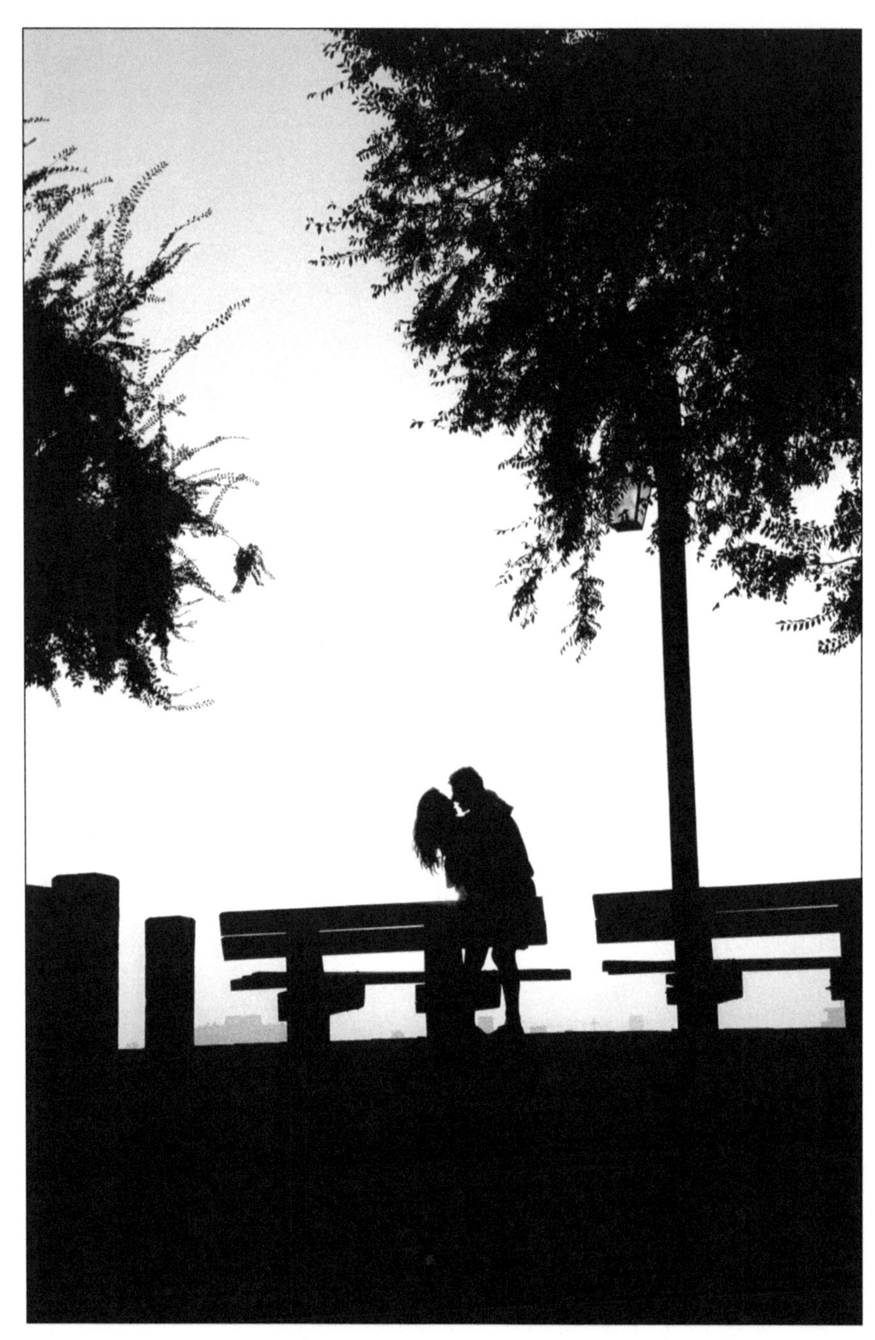

Lovers on the Mississippi Riverwalk
New Orleans, Louisiana 1990

Being in the Moment

Two lovers form a silhouette
in the halo
of the southern sunset,

heads tilting, eyes smiling,
arms hugging
for a soulful presence.

She's the crescent moon
throbbing
with his heartbeat,

and he Lake Pontchartrain
rocking her
into a mooring boat.

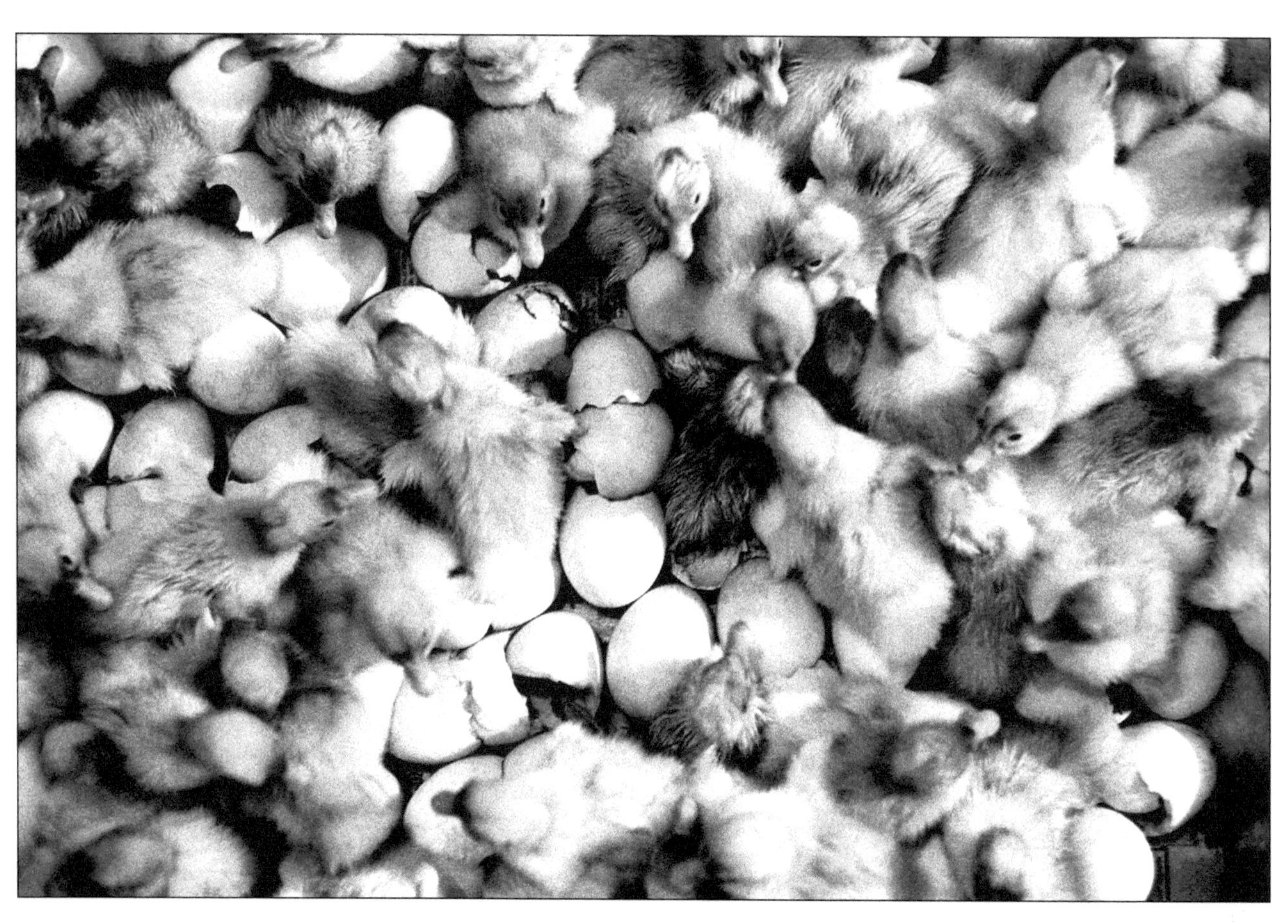

Barnhardt Duck Farm
Urbanna, Virginia 1970

Life Cycles

As soon as we hatch by breaking open our shells, we must realize the human dream of growing into a slaughter weight at an Olympic record-breaking speed, from fluffy ducklings to juveniles to adult ducks. Each day we long to quack by a pond where we can swim, bathe, splash, preen, head-bob or dabble with our bottoms up. But, confined as a breed raised for food on human dinner tables, we are crammed, thousands of us, in an indoor barn to live a short, caged life. We bump into each other without even a one-foot space to strut around. Manipulated by lighting and feed, all we do daily is eat-eat-eat and grow-grow-grow. Fed too much, we grow too fast. Our webbed feet barely support our overweight bodies. We must be diabetic and waddle with difficulty. Living in such depression, we feign a quacking cheerfulness. We know the time we close our eyes is when we are killed. Yet, we wonder whether our meat is a necessity for human health. Will our depression find a colony in their bodies? Perhaps they never care because they are crammed too, fighting each other here and there on Earth.

power outage
latest war news
turns black

cemetery visit
grass looks greener
around new tombs

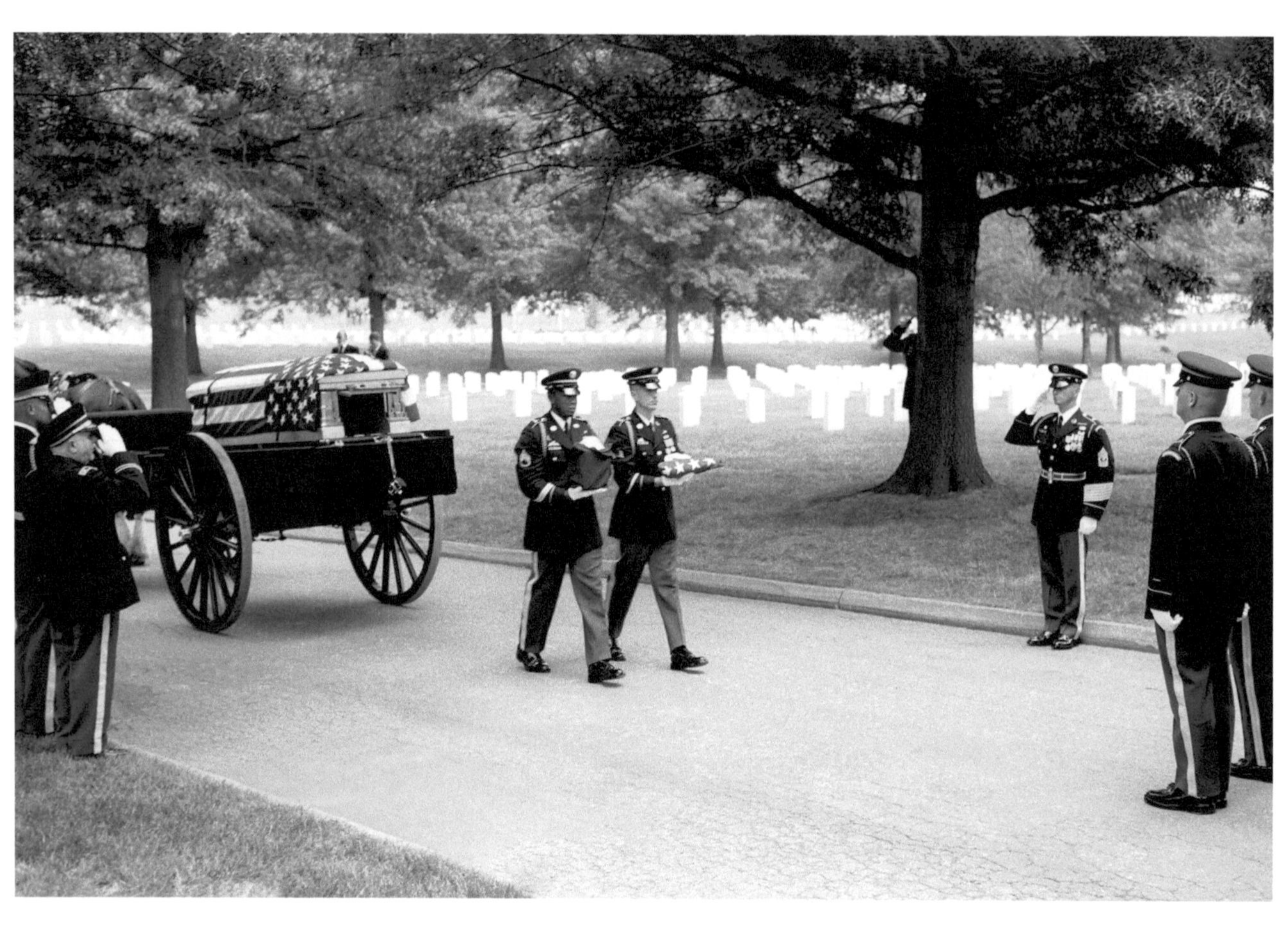

Lucein E. Conein's Funeral on Bastille Day
Arlington National Cemetery July 14, 1998

To Lou

Wherever we are, we share
the same sky, same earth,
same stars and stripes.

We met first in Saigon,
laughed and joked as if
the world was nothing

but a cue ball we hit
in our pool game. Once
I asked you in a dream if

we could gather again,
drink and eat in Saigon's
La Casita, and you,

squinting one eye,
answered with a grunt:
I'm at rest. Forever.

I drove over to see you
in Arlington, taking pictures
as my final salute.

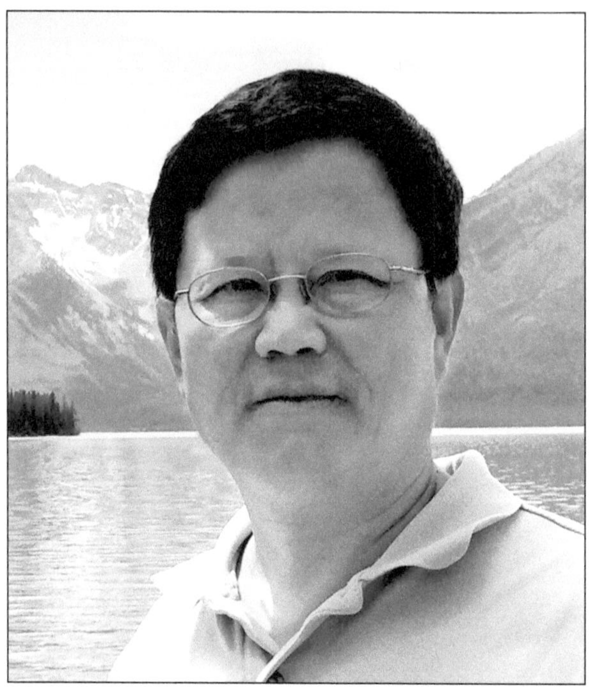

Jianqing Zheng is the author of *The Dog Years of Reeducation*, *A Way of Looking*, *The Landscape of the Mind*, *Enforced Rustication in the Chinese Cultural Revolution: Poems* and five poetry chapbooks and e-chapbooks.

He was the editor of seven scholarly books, including *Conversations with Dana Gioia* and *Sonia Sanchez's Poetic Spirit through Haiku,* and coeditor of four books, including *Dana Gioia: Poet & Critic*.

He received the 2019 Gerald Cable Book Prize, 2001 Slapering Hol Press Chapbook Award, and three poetry fellowships from the Mississippi Arts Commission, among other awards and honors.

He has published twenty photo essays in journals, including Arkansas Review, Fireflies' Light, Intégrité, Mississippi Folklife, The Right Words, and The Southern Quarterly. His book of haiku and photographs is *Delta Sun*.

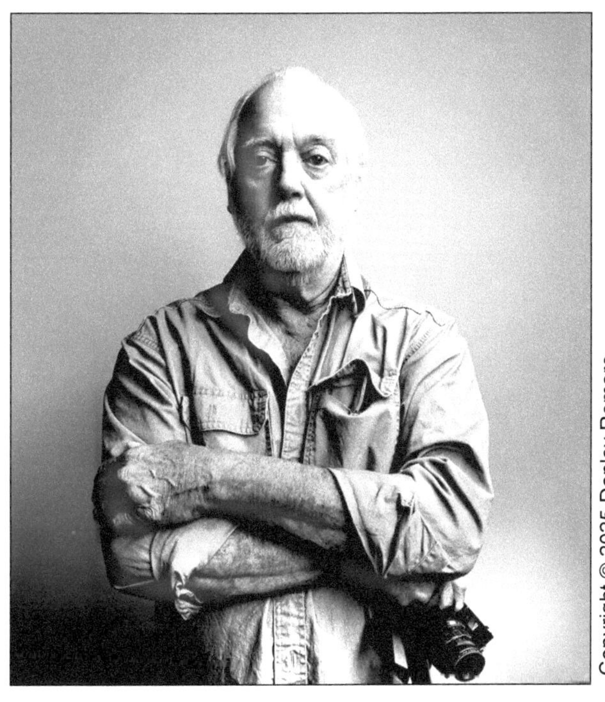
Copyright © 2025 Danley Romero

Leo Touchet has been photographing for over 50 years for numerous publications, corporations and for his personal street photography around the world.

Collections: The Sir Elton John Photography Collection, New Orleans Museum of Art, Houston Museum of Fine Arts, Hillliard Art Museum, Everson Museum, University of Maryland Baltimore, Bibliotheque National (France), Chase Manhattan Collection.

Publications: Life magazine, Time magazine, Fortune magazine, National Geographic Books, New York Times, Washington Post, Medical World News, Oxford American Magazine, Der Stern (Germany), Panorama (Italy), Popular Photography.

Exhibitions: His photographs have been displayed in over thirty museums, universities and galleries in the United States, Canada and France.
Books and Monographs: *Rejoice When You Die, Children Among Us, People Among Us, Flowers in Black & White, Chasing Shadows-Desert Sand Dunes, The Life of a Duck, At The Races,* and *Duet - Poet and Photographer.*

Acknowledgments

Jianqing Zheng would like to thank Leo for his photographic inspiration and the editors of the Delta Poetry Review, The Wise Owl, Verse-Virtual, and WCP Magazine for publishing some poems collected in this book.

Leo Touchet would like to thank Jianqing for suggesting that we work together on this book and he would also like to thank his wife Elizbeth Burk for years of support in all of his projects.

ISBN 979-8-9918323-1-1
90000>
9 798991 832311

www.ingramcontent.com/pod-product-compliance
Lightning Source LLC
LaVergne TN
LVHW070147110826
845147LV00002B/343
* 9 7 9 8 9 9 1 8 3 2 3 1 1 *